T0149342

Walking the Rails

My Childhood in Whitehall

Ethel Erickson Radmer

iUniverse, Inc.
Bloomington

Walking the Rails
My Childhood in Whitehall

iUniverse books may be ordered through booksellers or by contacting:

iUniverse
1663 Liberty Drive
Bloomington, IN 47403
www.iuniverse.com
1-800-Authors (1-800-288-4677)

ISBN: 978-1-4759-1008-7 (sc)
ISBN: 978-1-4759-1010-0 (hc)
ISBN: 978-1-4759-1009-4 (e)

Library of Congress Control Number: 2012906097

Printed in the United States of America

iUniverse rev. date: 4/11/2012

Front cover drawing by Ethel's grandson, Asher Smith.
Front cover graphics design by Tammy Radmer.

Unless otherwise noted, all photographs are courtesy of Ethel's personal collection. Photograph of author on back cover and photograph in Preface by Tammy Radmer.

All Bible quotes are from the King James Version of the Bible.

The author referenced and quoted from her dad's *Autobiography of Arvid B. Erickson*, as well as from his letters and essays. She also referenced and quoted from her mother Sarah's letters and her diaries—1938 and 1939 and from 1941 to 1950 (diaries of other years are missing). She has kept original punctuation and grammar, as written by Sarah and Arvid in their writings, in all direct quotes in the book.

The author gives much gratitude to her parents, now deceased.

Many thanks go to her sister Leone and a few other relatives and friends, including Rita, for conversing about the past when she had questions.

Contents

Preface

My daughter and her two children from San Francisco spent two weeks with me in a house I rented in Beloit, Wisconsin, in the summer of 2008. Though a resident of North Carolina, I was on a self-imposed, seven-month, unofficial writing stint at Beloit College, less than a mile from the Illinois border, to finish my third book. My grandson was a student at this "college that changes lives," according to one college guidebook, and he was happy to have me nearby. Plus, I wanted to see him and give him the chance to see our Wisconsin relatives.

My California family of three, all seasoned travelers, flew out in July. Tammy, eight-year-old Kai, ten-year-old Melia, and I enjoyed the pastoral campus with its towering oak and maples, leaping and running over and around Indian burial mounds and swimming in the pool where the students would swim, and then, while my grandson was busy with a full schedule of summer classes, the rest of us drove up to my hometown of Whitehall.

I was born and raised to college age in that small town of 1,035, the county seat of Trempealeau County.

We drove up in a rental car on a beautiful day just warm and humid enough to imbue us with a carefree abandon—light clothes, no encumbrances, and thoughts of fun and frolic. We were off on yet another merry adventure.

Through dairy farms spread alongside country roads and fields of corn and hay to feed the cattle we cruised.

Our young-hearted family of four loved everything: the red barns, black and white Holstein cows, and the brown and white Guernseys. "Yes, your Grandpa Carl was raised on a farm with Holsteins and proud of it," I said to the kids, "across this state of Wisconsin in Birnamwood, of Shakespeare fame."

But I, Carl's future wife, was brought up in a town—with a county courthouse, to boot—and I visited the farms of my friends.

In the middle of the western side of the state, not far from the Mississippi, and after four hours on the road from Beloit, we approached the town going north on Highway 53.

My hometown of Whitehall is nestled in a coulee, a region of depressions and high mounds left over from the skimming and droppings of glaciers ten thousand years ago—or, as my dad would say, "many mounds and hills that dotted the landscape and erected in some manner by the glaciers that made their way over the land during prehistoric times."

"There's the Whitehall sign," we all called. Population: 1,651. It had grown by 616 people since I grew up there. Decades ago, this had been my world.

We drove past old, handsome houses that I still knew and to the First Baptist Church, which I did not know any longer—a completely different building from my youth. But it stood on the same foundation of yesteryear's picturesque, white-clapboard frame with a square belfry that I had known intimately as a kid. "How firm a foundation," I thought, humming the hymn to myself. Those people had been like my second family.

We all got out and walked around. Then, a few blocks away, we looked at my old, used-to-be-yellow and now green stucco house. No one answered the door, so we climbed the evergreen trees, like I had done as a child, and we searched for the old lilac bushes.

The Green Bay and Western Railway Depot, built in 1914 and well preserved with a red brick facade, beckoned us with its ribbon of tracks that we could see a couple of blocks away. Whitehall's Depot had survived, while other depots across the country had been demolished. And to ensure its life and history, the depot was certified to be on the National Register of Historic Places in 2006. A volunteer let us in, and we talked about the old days, when my father was the depot agent and telegrapher for twenty-nine years, 1925–1954.

I showed Melia and Kai and Tammy how I walked the rails as a kid, and they took to it with abandon, way outpacing my steps, tentative to get the feel again on this steel balance beam. They swung foot over foot on the narrow rail just like I had when I was their age.

What joy we all exuded. Merriment was in the air for all our exploring the rest of the day.

We left Whitehall with Tammy at the wheel, driving us past more sloping green pastureland without end. Red barns, chicken coops, and cows dotted the landscape.

The kids were quiet. All of us were feeling the glow of time well spent.

Then Melia, leaning forward from the backseat, spoke up with a child's enthusiasm. "Grandma, I think you should write your next book about your childhood in Whitehall."

I was quiet for a few moments, my eyes becoming moist with tears as I choked up from the tenderness of her request. I turned my head back to her from the front passenger seat, her eager face meeting mine.

"Oh, Melia," I warbled back. "What a wonderful idea. I'm so touched that you want me to do that."

And that was how this book was born.

A Girl Was Born

"In the fall of 1935, when 'the frost was on the pumpkin, and the fodder was in the shock;' when the green leaves were changing their colors to the many golden hues of Autumn; when Mother Nature was singing her lullaby to her brood in preparation for a long winter's slumber of hibernation in accordance with her Cyclic Laws, an event of great importance took place on November 6th 1935 at 12:30 High Noon; an individual in a small physical body was born into our world of storm and strife, albeit a world of beauty and order and system; born as a female in our house and we called her Ethel Mae. What a name! What a girl!" This was my dad's welcome for my arrival, written in his autobiography.

I came on a Wednesday and weighed in at 9½ pounds on the "fisherman's scale" that the doctor brought to my parents' home. I was laid onto a blanket with rings on a hook and a weight measure needle at the top. Dr J C Tyvand, the physician who held me as I came out of my mother Sarah's womb, was assisted by nurse Mrs. J. C. Tyvand. It was a normal, natural birth, with my mother lying in her own bed, gently pushing me out the birth canal to introduce me to life outside my nourishing cocoon of nine months. I came to rest in my mother's arms against her breast.

Ah! What peace and love and adventure I felt from birth on through all my years growing up in Whitehall, Wisconsin. What good fortune I had to have caring, nurturing parents in a very manageable town of 1,035 to know and explore with ease and safety, filled with people who knew and cared about me and whom I in turn could trust and churches to inspire some morals and ethics.

In the center of my town of birth and in the center of our lives was the Green Bay and Western Railway Depot. The continuous ribbon of two parallel railroad tracks ran straight through the middle of the town and right through the middle of the state of Wisconsin, cutting it in half horizontally as it connected town to town east and west. We rode the trains across the state and walked those rails into the countryside surrounding my hometown, where we could roam freely and with abandon.

My mother was forty-six years old when she had me, and I was fortunate to not be a statistic for higher birth defects in children born to mothers over forty, higher still among first-time mothers. But I was not her first! My mother had at least ten pregnancies in her fertile life—seven survived through adulthood, two died young, and one miscarried. I was the last that I knew of of her conceptions. What a relief that must have been! And she seemed to show it with a grateful ease about life. She could sit back in her Mission Style, oak-stained wood and brown leather rocking chair and relax with me, enjoying the fruits of her labors at birth and in rearing her brood. I was a good girl all the way, as it turned out, and on occasion, she called me that.

The Wisconsin Department of Health's Bureau of Vital Statistics wanted to know for the birth record if I was legitimate. Yes. The mother's full maiden name was Sarah Larson. (Her parents' generation of regular folks did not give their children middle names.) And the father was A. B Erickson. (He gave himself a middle initial "B" without a period because he liked the acronym ABE, signifying honest Abe, or Abraham Lincoln.) For color or race, father and mother were both "W" for White. Both were forty-six at their last birthday. The father's trade, profession, or particular kind of work done (as spinner, sawyer, bookkeeper, etc.) was railroad depot agent. My mother's trade, profession, or particular kind of work done (as housekeeper, typist, nurse, clerk, etc.) was housewife. The industry or business in which work was done (as silk mill, sawmill, bank, lawyer's office or own home) was not answered. And for the record, a sawyer worked in a sawmill and a spinner worked in a silk mill (or a midwestern or northeastern textile mill for flax, linen and wool—cotton mills were in the South) spinning silk thread from a silkworm cocoon. The eggs and cocoons came from China and Japan (until World War II started) and were transported by my dad's lifetime love, the rails, across the United States. Spinners found the beginning of the silk thread in the cocoon and unraveled it as it was wound onto a spindle. The thread was then made into a warp and woven into cloth to make silk stockings, hankies, caps, panties, dresses, scarves, ribbons, and embroidery thread, all of which our family used, plus some of my baby clothes. I owe thanks to the seven hundred perfect silkworm cocoons that it takes to make one silk baby dress. Silk parachutes we did not use, nor the silk kites the frugal Ben Franklin splurged on for his famous electricity experiments. We were consumers of silk, but we were not spinners, and there weren't any spinners nearby. The closest textile mills were in Milwaukee, where flax and linen were also spun. Those textile mills of yesteryear are now museums and funky locales for businesses. Sawyers, however, were close by in neighboring Jackson County, which was full of Jackson Pine. Sawyers were vital in the lumber mill business for which Wisconsin was famous. My grandpa, Nels Erickson, who was my father's father and who died five years before I was born, was a sawyer and a lumberjack and helped keep those mills filled with huge trunks of pine and fir. The sawyers sawed them into planks for the burgeoning construction demands in a growing state and nation in the early-to-mid-1900s.

Was 1 percent silver nitrate used to prevent infant blindness? Was child deformed or physically defective? Nature of the defect? The questions were left unanswered. And I appeared normal in every way.

The top of the Certificate of Birth Registration said, "The world of tomorrow is in the hands of the children of today." Yes, the future's changes were in my hands and the hands of others to come. For one, all those professions and trades listed on my birth certificate and typical at the time to one gender or the other would be infiltrated with both sexes. Some jobs faded with diminished need or were melded with other skills to make a new trade or profession.

But medical doctors were always in demand. People got sick, and babies were being born, including me. Dr. Tyvand's bill for $22 arrived in the mail on November 30, and my father paid it promptly in cash that Saturday in the doctor's office. Our family kept no debts. My parents paid cash for our new house in 1930 and for our new Ford four-door sedan from Auto Sales in Whitehall in 1934 (a year before I was born), when few people were buying new cars, to replace Dad's used Chevrolet of 1929. Before the Chevrolet, he drove a "Star" touring car that he bought from a dealer for $300 in April 1923. We paid cash for our health care or anything else with a dollar sign on it. I was home free and paid for.

I was born into a family of seven children: Benjamin Ward was twenty years old, Raymond Arvid was seventeen, Sherman Bernarr was thirteen, Myron Dallas was eleven, Avis Marie was nine, Leone Arvis was four, and I brought up the rear. The two grown-up kids were off to the university and jobs, and the four who were still around welcomed me into our family, genuinely happy to have a baby in the house again. Years later, my brother Ray spoke fondly of watching and listening to our mother in her rocking chair, holding and nursing me while softly singing Swedish songs.

The townspeople welcomed me too. Mother's church group, the Dorcas Society, wrote the sweetest of poems in the swirliest of scripts.

Welcome, baby dear!
Wee little ears and
a snub of a nose,
almost no hair
and tiniest toes,
Wee little bundle of
sunshine and cheer—
Welcome, sweet treasure.
We're so glad you're here!

Neighbors, friends, and relatives came steadily to our two-story yellow stucco house on the corner of Blair and West Streets, from the day of my birth and over the next month, bringing gifts. My mother was of such a calm, good nature that she received the company with grace. Her mother, Sarah, and her sister, Ruth, stayed for several weeks to help with chores, though my mom still had her hands full and must have been tired. But she was quietly proud to show off her new, plump baby, whom she loved tenderly.

My mother, a conscientious record keeper, wrote down in family records the names of her visitors and the gifts they brought. All the married women were called by their husbands' names. Mrs. Arne Rasmussen, from a big farmhouse and farmland on the edge of town, came over for a visit and to admire this child only hours after I was born.

Mrs. Sig Hegge, our neighbor across the street in perhaps the biggest house and biggest lot in town, brought over a batch of good donuts the next morning, made in her own kitchen. When I grew into a kid and could go to my friend Patty Hegge's house to play, I saw Mrs. Hegge put pressed circles of dough with a hole in the center into a pan of hot lard a couple inches deep, and when the donuts rose to the surface, she turned them over with a fork, took them out, and rested them on brown paper or a dish towel to soak up the excess oil. I remember them tasting dense from the fat, but sweet.

Mrs. Hallie Wright came with a nice pink rubber pantie of rayon for the light pink baby. Elsie Mae Johnson, a schoolteacher from across Blair Street, brought Ethel Mae a rattle and a rubber doll that my family called Elsie Mae.

That added to the three rubber dolls my family gave me made for what my mother said was "a nice family of rubber dolls."

Mrs. Leonard Jorgenson sent baby a nice wool sweater for ninety-eight cents and a silk bonnet for forty-nine cents, both in baby blue to match my eyes. The tags were still on in case they needed exchanging.

Both Mrs. Talg and Mrs. F. Billman gave baby silk kimono goods for my mom to sew dresses and jackets for me, when she regained her strength, on her shuttle Singer sewing machine in a treadle stand in her bedroom during the winter months. In the summer she moved the Singer out onto the closed-in porch in the front of our house.

To top it off, I got my first penny. "ONE CENT" and "UNITED STATES OF AMERICA" are stamped on one side, with two shafts of wheat wrapped along the side edges of bright copper and "E PLURIBUS UNUM" along the top. The other side, with President Lincoln's head and torso in profile and my birth year, 1935, to the side, remains unseen. My dad preserved it in my baby book under a seal that I have never broken.

The Wm. Wrigley Jr. Company of Chicago, Illinois, sent me in December, a month after I was born, a nice letter and my first stick of Wrigley's gum and, like my copper penny still sealed under cellophane, the gum is still sealed in foil and cellophane. They mistook me for older when they said, "And at two years, you are just about old enough to enjoy Wrigley's gum ... I think you will like the long-lasting, sweet, juicy flavor." They also said:

> It is fine for children and good for children's teeth, which need more exercise than they get with modern soft food. Maybe your mother doesn't know this, and so be sure to tell her. Your mother always wants to know about everything that is for your good.
> Your friend,
> The Wrigley Spearman
>
> P.S. If you still have a few teeth to come through, chewing Wrigley's gum will help you.

I didn't become a sweet-gum chewer, thank goodness, but later the sugar of occasional Three Musketeers candy bars did take a toll on my six-year molars, which were extracted when I was a teenager. Drilling and filling might have done the job instead, but dentists were not as skilled then, and pulling a tooth out was easier. I did have a few teeth left and a few teeth to come through—my wisdom teeth, to make me wiser in my choosing to not eat many sweets and to brush my teeth after eating.

I was born into the Great Depression and the events leading to World

War II. My dad, in his written welcome to me, had said I "was born into our world of storm and strife." That was so true, but I, the infant, didn't know it. Many people lost their jobs and their savings. But we were lucky that Dad had a steady job as depot agent and telegrapher, made even more important by the need for the delivery of vital goods and news during hard times and building up to war. So we were able to stay in our house, buy and grow our food as my father and mother always had, and provide for other needs. Our parents thanked the good Lord for it, and Mother showed her compassion for others in need with meals for the hungry that appeared at our back doorstep. The "tramps" as they were called traveled the trains, hitching a ride in a boxcar as the train came whipping by. They grabbed a handrail on the outside of any of the train cars if they were speedy enough, or if the train was going slowly, they reached for the outstretched arm of another helpful "bum" leaning over from inside the boxcar. And they were off to the next town and the next, a virtual network for survival. The tramps hopped off and on the trains outside of town in order to not be seen. The railroad only allowed paying passengers and would have had the police arrest the nonpaying tramps if they were caught. They gathered in a grove of trees outside of town near the County Mental Hospital on the hill to sleep and to cook over a fire. When they ventured into town, they knew where to go. Ours was a marked house. A large "X" was drawn by the tramps with a white stone on the front, gray cement foundation that could be seen a block away. And with my mother's goodness—she prepared a plate of scrambled eggs, fried home-grown potatoes, and homemade bread with butter and a piece of home-baked cake, accompanied by a cup of hot coffee with cream—her house was known on the traveling railroad grapevine as a safe place for food. I learned about this as I grew into a child, and I remember standing at our pantry screen door in the back of our house, as my older sister Leone did, and looking out at these quiet, polite men eating on our back stoop. My mother tried to scrub the "X" away to not draw too much attention, but it would reappear.

There was hardship among the residents of the town as well, years before I was born. Mary Louise's dad, Mr. Hughitt Johnson, lost his job and joined the Civilian Conservation Corporation, or CCC, camp that the government set up to give people work and the chance to make a little money. The one bank in town, owned and run by Mr. H. Hegge, collapsed. The assets dried up and disappeared, and people didn't get their money. He had just enough left to buy a feed mill and then use the income to pay ten cents on the dollar, as was required by law, back to the people who had lost their money. At least it was something to help with their losses, and Mr. Sig Hegge was honest and hardworking to try to make amends. More kindness came from Dr. Tyvand, who saw patients for free if they couldn't afford to pay him.

People were quiet about their hardship. They didn't wear their plight on their sleeve. They felt embarrassed and humiliated and frightened, not traits you wanted to let others see or know about. They tried hard to work their way out of it and would take any job, however menial.

The Great Depression originated in the United States with the stock market crash of October 29, 1929, known as Black Tuesday, six years before I was born. It had already spread to almost every country in the world when it hit the United States. Many countries set up relief programs, and most underwent some sort of political upheaval, pushing them to the left or right. In some countries, the citizens turned toward nationalist demagogues, the most infamous being Adolf Hitler. The Depression lasted for a decade and faded with the advent of World War II in 1939, when I was 3½ years old. The massive rearmament buildup of the United States and of Europe and Great Britain leading up to WWII helped stimulate those economies. America's late entry into the war in 1941 finally eliminated the last effects from the Great Depression.

Franklin Delano Roosevelt was president of the United States when I was born, and Adolf Hitler was the leader of Germany. The first concentration camp existed, having opened at Dachau in 1934, the year before my birth. The Nuremberg Race Laws stripped German Jews of their rights. And a year after my birth, German troops occupied the Rhineland, covering the whole demilitarized German region to the west of the Rhine River. Benito Mussolini's Italian forces showed their aggression by taking Ethiopia, and civil war erupted in Spain. And unbeknownst to me, the contented babe in a homemade cradle, the war was building up to even more tumultuous times.

In 1939, the Nazis took Czechoslovakia and invaded Poland. The Russians also invaded Poland, in addition to Lithuania, Latvia, and Estonia, and attacked Finland. The United States proclaimed neutrality, while Canada chose to follow Britain and France in declaring war on Germany.

I was four years old when the Nazis invaded Denmark, Norway, the Netherlands, Belgium, Luxembourg, and France, and Winston Churchill became British prime minister. I'm guessing that our parents might have felt quiet admiration and relief, though they didn't show it openly, when Sweden, where my parents' cousins still lived, remained neutral.

A year later, at the end of 1941, the United States and Britain declared war on Japan, and Germany declared war on the United States. The first American forces arrived in Great Britain in 1942 and then fought on European soil. Germany's expansion into Soviet territory was reversed at Stalingrad in 1943.

There were other attacks, captures, and surrenders in 1944, and the Nazi concentration camps were liberated in 1945. Roosevelt died, Truman became president, and Hitler committed suicide all in the month of April 1945. Victory in Europe, V-E Day, was declared in May 1945.

There was more to come that year, when the United States, by executive order of President Harry S. Truman, dropped the first atomic bomb on Hiroshima, Japan, on August 6 and a second bomb on Nagasaki on August 9. Japan surrendered unconditionally that same month. The Nuremberg Trials of war crimes began, and the United Nations was born. There was hope with the coming together of countries in a forum that the cataclysm of wars would not dominate our lives again.

The events of the 1930s and 1940s were dizzying, and the repercussions lasted decades. Who would have imagined so many countries at war, such destructive weaponry, and the massacres of millions of human beings?

Two of my brothers and many of their buddies, several barely out of high school, enlisted or were drafted in that war. Dallas was handsome in his Marine Corps uniform, and he sent letters from Peleliu Island, part of New Hebrides, a relatively safe outpost of the war in the South Pacific, and though he was in a foxhole and shot at, he escaped. Sherman in India, looking tall and confident in his khaki cotton army fatigues and garrison cap, sent me, when I was ten years old, three rupees and what we called "Aladdin slippers." When I saw the slippers, I wrote in my diary that they also reminded me of pictures of lanterns at the end of the shoes in Bible times. "Please God, show us and light the way," is what my mother would say, "out of war and to a place of peace."

I was too young to know much about war. As a toddler, I remember seeing my parents sitting in their respective chairs, listening to their RCA Victor tabletop radio, the tall, brown wooden cabinet embellished with fluted trim on the front, the sides and the rounded crown coming to a high point, waiting for news of the war and listening to President Truman's voice, strong and forceful, coming out of the speaker. As parents, they were worried but proud to have two sons in the war. Several of their friends did not make it back from the war, and all were remembered on the "Roll of Honor" next to city hall.

On the national scene, there were other less momentous events than the Depression and the buildup to the war that happened the year of my birth and interested my mother enough for her to clip newspaper articles and glue them in large scrapbooks. Will Rogers, the humorist, and Wiley Post met their deaths in a plane crash in Arctic Alaska three months before my birth. John D. Rockefeller Sr., the oil king, turned ninety-six and said he expected to reach one hundred (he reached ninety-seven).

The Dionne quintuplets, the only known female identical set of five in the world, celebrated their first birthday in July 1935 in a hospital in Toronto, Ontario, Canada. Cecile Marie Emilda, Yvonne Edouilda Marie, Emilie Marie Emilda, Marie Reine Alma, and Annette Lillianne Marie, each one with four names rather than my mother's generation of two. By law they were made wards of the king for nine years. The government made money off them as a spectacle, as thousands of people a day stood on an observation gallery surrounding their playground and watched them play. Their parents grieved for them until they won back custody in November 1943, when the girls were nine years old and I was eight.

Bruno Hauptmann, a German carpenter, was found guilty on February 13, 1935, of first-degree murder of the twenty-month-old son of the famous pilots, Charles and Anne Lindbergh. Charles Jr. was kidnapped from their home on the evening of March 1, 1932, and found dead two months later just two miles away in the woods. The press at the time called it "the crime of the century." Hauptmann was sentenced to die in the electric chair and was executed in 1936. That might have struck fear in my mother's heart, as she posted several articles about the kidnapping and the trial in her scrapbooks, but I was safe and sound, and unlike the five identical Dionne sisters who were taken by the king, I was secure at home with my parents.

Aimee Semple McPherson, whom my parents saw and heard in Los Angeles while on a vacation, was a charismatic evangelist, famous and infamous and the founder of the Church of the Foursquare Gospel and of the Angelus Temple. She drew crowds to her services and then made headlines that my mother posted in her scrapbooks with courtroom divorce proceedings in 1934 from her third husband David Hutton. She was a strong, independent, talented woman and was known as a pioneer in the use of modern media. Feminists today could view her independence and strength with admiration. On September 26, 1944, almost nine years after my birth, we heard on the radio that Mrs. Aimee McPherson died.

Two Washington scientists were issued a patent in August 1935 for developing the first device for applying color to transmitted moving pictures with light passing through quartz. It was vital in the development of color television. The 1939 World's Fair was a showcase for the first televised presidential speech, telecast on RCA's new line of television receivers and inaugurating regular scheduled TV broadcasting in New York City. About one thousand people throughout the NYC area saw President Franklin Delano Roosevelt's address. Albert Einstein also gave a speech about cosmic rays. I wish I had heard and seen him, even at my young age of 3½ years.

So the world I was being introduced to was not just "a world of storm and strife," in my Dad's words, but "a world of beauty and order and system"

9

as well, with technology on the rise and scientific theories and research exploding. Beauty is in the eye of the beholder, and I see a lot of it looking back on those carefree, happy, simpler days of my innocent youth in my hometown of Whitehall. And unlike what Thomas Wolfe's novel tells us, I say yes, you can go home again.

Walking, Climbing, Falling

I THRIVED IN THOSE early years. The house was full of activity with a family of nine, plus frequent and long visits from my mother's mother and sisters. There was no lack of entertainment or help or learning. We had no television or telephone. Dad took pleasure in reading the "funny papers" to us from the Milwaukee Journal on Sundays after church. "The Katzenjammer Kids," "Dagwood," and other comic strips amused all of us. My brother Sherman, sixteen years old at the time, taught me how to write my name when I was almost four. He, a lefty, but forced by his teacher to hold his paper and pencil in a righty position, wrote my name with his left hand held in a twisted, upside down position that he used all his life. I wrote my name by following his writing, but my right hand was held in a "normal" position, my writing all in clear capital letters that have been saved through the decades.

When I was a year and twenty-three days old, I walked across the room, with my dad watching and without his help, thirty-seven steps in all. At the same time, I started to climb up on chairs. No first step was ever recorded—just that I started to move around on my rear, by the seat of my pants. I must have been saving up the steps for a dramatic moment. But, as in so much that life hands us, that prowess set me up for a fall—or falls.

Four months later, I climbed up the long, wooden stairway of fifteen steps (this house had high ceilings) to the upstairs, all alone, and ran from one room to another, full of excitement. The next day I did it again and fell halfway down the stairs backward (some people didn't gate their stairs back then). I was not deterred. A few days later, while Dad and I were home alone

11

upstairs, I fell down the stairs again, this time the whole length, and landed on my face. A metal in-floor register at the bottom of the stairs provided no cushion. One eye was black and blue for several weeks. At two years, I bruised my forehead badly when I fell on the cement sidewalk, and at three years old, I fell out of the trapeze swing on our lawn right on my knees and nose. Dad washed me up and put a rag on my bruises. He recorded those falls in my baby book on the page across from my first prayer. Ma, as I called her in my early years, along with "Mother" and "Mom," made sure that I said that first prayer every night until I grew into making up my own prayers. "Now I lay me seepy. Amen," at first. Later, "Now I lay me down to sleep. I pray the Lord my soul to keep. If I should die before I wake, I pray the Lord my soul to take. Amen." My morning prayer was "Dear Jesus, I pray thee for help through the day to keep pure and clean like the snow my thoughts and my actions, my words and my play. Be with me wherever I go. Amen."

Maybe it was all that praying that helped my body recover. Thank God for the resilience of a toddler. If the falls made for any long-term damage to my brain, my parents didn't see it or say it, and I will never know. It's probably best that way. I'm sure there were many falls to come—even as adults we fall. As Jeannette Walls, author of *The Glass Castle*, says in her talks, paraphrased by me, we fall and fall again, even with lots of bruises, and we don't need to feel ashamed. It's okay, and we are glad to learn—even better with the marks and bruises—so much more about life and being able to live it.

I also survived a near poisoning. My mother was in the basement with me nearby, washing clothes in her wringer washing machine. She had to hand feed the washed clothes through the hand wringer into the two-bin rinse water basin and put them through the ringer again and again. Then she hung the clothes up to dry either on the basement clotheslines or outside if it wasn't raining. I was about two and sitting on a small, wheeled toy with handles called a "kiddy car." I saw a jar with clear liquid in it and reached up and had a drink. It was not water, but kerosene! My mother saw me cough and sputter—kerosene tastes bad—and acted fast. I was breathing okay. She kept a First Aid clipping with "Poisons taken internally" on the list. If she followed it, she would have checked my mouth and throat for burns, then given me an emetic like soda in warm water to encourage vomiting (a questionable thing to do today) and hope that my body would clear out the poison. I recovered quickly with no apparent bad effects. If there was any damage done to my body parts, I think it has repaired itself. My dad clipped a newspaper article from the Milwaukee Journal of another toddler in Milwaukee, lucky to be alive after drinking kerosene. His mom administered artificial respiration, and a midwife friend took him to the hospital to have his stomach pumped. We were both lucky to be alive.

When I was sick my mother held me, sometimes for hours at a time. She recorded in her diary when I was two years old, on a freezing, two-above-zero Friday in January, that when I got up I was "not so well." Mother held me most of the morning until lunchtime, when I brightened up and was spry the rest of the day. On other days when I was feverish, she also held me for hours. At bedtime, Mother hoped baby would be all right by morning. On any evening, she would rock me to sleep and then read, do chores, or occasionally go to a quilting bee at Mrs. Rasmussen's house or a prayer meeting at the Baptist Church or the Tabernacle, with Dad and my siblings at home. I can imagine only good things came from such attention. We know that placing your hands upon a person can affect what is happening in their body. Human touch increases levels of growth hormones and reduces stress hormones, and it follows that immunity is enhanced. As a babe, what could be better than being kept close to your mother's heart?

But along with the loving attention also came a gift of freedom and independence. Our parents allowed us to be on our own a lot from a very young age. We figured things out by ourselves, though we knew we could ask our parents if we needed to. We roamed freely from a young age on, wandering around the town or going alone to a neighbor's house, our parents knowing it was safe, for the most part. We learned to trust ourselves. Freedom has its risks, but we all survived, and I think we were the better for it.

By age three, I sometimes went to bed by myself. As soon as I started walking, I played alone in our yard or with Leone, who was four years older than me. Sometimes I would walk to our neighbor next door, the Albert Stuve house, for a while to see Audrey, who was two years younger than me. When I was almost four years old, on a very nice and bright day, I told my mother that I was going to play with Patricia Hegge, across West Street. But Patricia was at school practicing for a play, and I decided to walk several blocks away and across the railroad tracks to the depot, where my dad worked, by myself. I'm sure my dad was surprised to see me, and I think my mother was quietly amused when she found out. And, showing some independence of thought, I spoke up for myself at a young age. Leone, seven, and I, three, were "scrapping," as my mother described it, about fruit nectar glasses, while Mother was canning pears. I guess we wanted to play with, sort, and admire the glasses that the other one did not want to give up. At last I gave in, but I had the last word with "Okay, baby Leone."

But, at about the same age, I didn't know what my teenage brothers were up to when they gave me a drink of their home-brewed "root beer," which my brothers brewed secretly in their bedroom closet upstairs. Mother didn't know until the carbonated beverage overflowed through the floor and to the living room ceiling below. It was a mess that Mother couldn't miss, and she probably had to clean up the damage. The boys moved the remainder of the batch to the basement. What Mother didn't know was that it might have been fermented. She was strongly opposed to drinking alcohol. Leone brought the tangy fizz in a glass bottle on a picnic with no effects that she remembered. Ray years later claimed with amusement that they once gave me a sip and I was tipsy. I wasn't amused when I heard that. I was just an innocent toddler beginning to learn about the world!

This was a busy household with seven kids, but my parents took it all in stride, never complaining, losing patience, or saying a harsh word. My dad had a more than full-time job at the depot as the agent and telegrapher, also doing any other depot jobs that needed doing. The extra work included being available around the clock and weekends for emergencies, building a large rack at his expense of money and time for the front of his car to deliver the freight and mail, and doing upkeep chores like oiling the depot floors. As we grew older, we kids all had our turn to help him out, "collecting" on Saturday mornings from businesses throughout the town whatever they owed the railroad.

But my mother was in charge at home, and the job was big. Unless she was really ill, she never failed in having three sit-down meals a day, either on the drop-leaf white pine table in the kitchen or on the large oak dining room table for the whole family. We mostly did not cook or fix meals for ourselves when we were young, though we helped her when she asked. She liked to have the kitchen to herself.

Her chores were endless: shopping every day for food, ordering clothes and other needs from mail-order catalogues; planting and tending to an organic garden at home and on plots of land owned by the Green Bay and Western on railroad track curves outside of town; canning many quarts of vegetables and fruits to store for the winter; tending to flowers growing outside and in; sewing quilts and clothes for all of us; mopping and sometimes varnishing floors and waxing them with Johnson's Glo Coat wax; sweeping the soot-covered basement ceiling and low hanging furnace pipes; washing ceilings, walls and windows every several months; spring cleaning lace curtains on a curtain stretcher outside; painting cupboards with varnish or shellac and painting linoleum floors with a sponge imprint (an opportunity to show her creativity) and putting a layer of varnish on top; keeping Charlie Schultz, the ice man, coming with ice for the ice box (until we bought a small refrigerator in January 1942); fixing fires in the kitchen stove for baking and cooking until we purchased a small electric stove with oven; shoveling coal and starting and stoking coal fires in the furnace from early morning to late at night; sharpening the hand-powered lawn mower blades and taking the wheel parts off to grease it up; washing everyone's clothes in a ringer washing machine, including for Ben who was a traveling fill-in depot agent and Ray studying chemical engineering at the University of Wisconsin in Madison and shipping laundry boxes back and forth in the mail; hanging clothes on the outside clothesline or in the basement; ironing clothes and muslin sheets; baking ten loaves of bread at a time and cakes and pies frequently; entertaining visiting relatives with meals and a place to sleep; giving us kids attention when we needed it at school, with a doctor visit, or at church; and keeping the peace if it was needed by being peaceful herself.

All through my toddler-hood, my ma, as my mother had called her own mother, and I walked downtown almost every day, twice a day. This is how I learned about the world. We went to the Farmer's Store, six blocks away, on Main Street for groceries and walked past the Pontiac Dealer on the corner of Scranton and Abrams Streets to Foss's Market for meat and primost, a sweet Scandinavian cheese to put on our Swedish hardtack for an easy, back-to-our-roots supper. We bought packages of colored sugar at four cents a package to decorate the top of frosting, an angel cake for thirty-nine cents, a case of peaches for ninety-eight cents and three delicious apples from Washington state for ten cents. My dad ate one every day, peeling and slicing and handing slices to us at the dining table, saying, "An apple a day keeps the doctor away." We paid ten cents for a pound of butter if we didn't get it at the creamery near our house. Mother got some heavy sugar sacks with stripes on at Erickson's Store for five cents each and Daniel Webster flour by the barrel that Dad or Sherm would pick up later in the car. She always looked for day-old baked goods at the Whitehall Bakery, next to what became Fortun's Drug Store on Main Street. Eleven cupcakes and five rolls cost her ten cents. Our favorite, Bismarcks and Long Johns, round and rectangular donuts filled with jam or chocolate sauce and frosted with white powdered sugar frosting, were a bargain price of just pennies. At Van Gordon's Feed Store, she bought one bushel of snow apples for $1.19 and one forty-nine-pound sack of Country Girl flour that included a free dish towel for $1.00, to be picked up by Dad in his car. We purchased boxes of hand soap, a three pound can of coffee for eighty-two cents and lemon pie filling in a box from the Jewel Tea man who came to our door, plus the Jewel Tea Autumn Leaf pattern china that filled our glass fronted, built-in-the-wall kitchen cabinet.

We passed the Wisconsin Bell Telephone Company office, housed in a small, white, wood-sided building on Dewey Street, on our way to the depot. Sometimes Mother would stop in and say hello to Mrs. Stuve, the switchboard operator. We did not have a telephone at home, so we did not have a bill to pay. Mrs. Stuve talked with callers on a headset with earphones and a mouthpiece in order to keep her hands free. She sat in front of a black, wooden, vertical panel filled with rows of holes and jacks. Her arms rested on a horizontal console that held a rotary dialer and thirty or more cords with metal knobs on the ends to pull out and plug into the holes on the panel. That connected the caller to the person being called. The operator not only had a technical job operating the equipment, testing lines, and even splicing a cable if needed, but she was also the center of information. Here was a chance for her and the person on the line to find out the time and to catch or pass on a bit of gossip or news. This personal attention was stricken with phone company rules when automatic dialing systems took hold later in the '50s. Almost all the 350,000 switchboard operators in the United States in the '40s were women. Slowly they were phased out, moving on to other jobs or returning to homemaking.

Our next stop was the depot. Mother wrote letters—then both a prolific art form and a practical way to communicate without a phone—in Dad's office, and Dad put them in the mail sacks that he collected to put on the trains coming through at least twice a day. I loved being in the depot with my mom and dad. It was so natural that they were working together. They were a business team managing a family. I watched Dad as he operated the telegraph transmitter, called a "key" or "bug," and we both listened to the pleasant rat-a-tat of telegraph dots and dashes coming in on the receiver, also called a "sounder." I tried to make sense of the sounds, which were deciphered easily and instantaneously by my dad as letters and words. He might send a message to Ben at the depot in New London or in Arcadia to say that Mother and I were in the office and to ask when he would be coming home next. He would click a dot, a dash, four dots, another dot, and a long dash to spell out "Ethel." He signed off with "seventy-three," the sign for "best regards" in International Morse. I also roamed the large waiting rooms, one for women and one for men (though that didn't hold in practice), and went outdoors on the cement platform to watch for the steam engines pulling trains or the section gang coming through on their hand carts, looking for and replacing bad ties, tamping loose spikes, and tightening bolts all along the tracks from Winona, Minnesota, to Green Bay, Wisconsin. My brothers did hard, hot work on those gangs in the summer months to earn money for college. It was not for the faint-hearted. You literally could faint with the heat and dehydration of heavy labor. Then we might stop in to see one of my mother's friends at their homes for a little lunch, and we walked back home to take a rest.

You wouldn't have known it, and we didn't really talk about it, but my mother was often not well. It wasn't an overt sickness or disease. She would simply say that she was not strong and needed to rest. She would go lie down on her bed, and the life of the family would go on as usual. Several times she sent a handkerchief in the mail to Dr. Charles S. Price, a famous evangelist whom my parents had seen and heard in a tent in Seattle, Washington, while on a vacation. He anointed and prayed over the handkerchief (and perhaps hundreds of others) and then returned it for her to place on her body. With the same idea of her holding and caressing me to help me feel better when I was feverish, she felt healing warmth and prayerful intentions from the "hands-on," blessed handkerchief. And other prayers from people coming to her home and from church "all really seemed to make me feel better," she said. Mother attended healing services at the Tabernacle. She saw Dr. Tyvand in his office or he came to the house if she was in bed. One noon hour when Dad was home for lunch, he called Dr. Tyvand to come over and see Mother, who was staying in bed upstairs for most of the day. He examined her and said she was overworked and run down and should stay in bed for several days. After I was born, she started to bleed a lot and took mint-flavored cod liver oil, which contained vitamin A, to help her red blood cells make hemoglobin and liver capsules that she ordered herself from Montgomery Ward & Co. for being "highly anemic," according to Dr. Tyvand. He recommended she have surgery for "piles" after her blood was built up. (Years later, she did have surgery to remove her uterus at the hospital where Leone was a nursing student.) Several nephews were staying in our house while she was in bed at home, and she asked that someone bring them to their homes in Garden Valley since she was unable to keep them any longer. One or another of her many sisters came to help. Friends came to the house to pray for Mother. Rev. Floyd Larson anointed her, and she said she felt such a sweet spirit in the prayer. Ray drove her to Garden Valley, where Grandma Sarah took over. Mother said, "I was sure treated kind by my mother and I had a good chance to rest and I slept good." After four days, Dallas, Avis, Leone, Aunt Ellen, and I all drove to see her, and our mother was glad to see us. At last, mustering up strength, she decided to go back home with us. And then she was back to being overworked.

I was just three years old when my mother took me to Arcadia, fourteen miles southwest of our town, on what I called the "passador" train. Mom bought a brown coat with brown wolf fur trim and collar and rayon lining for $2.98, marked down from $14.98, and a silk dress for $1.00, plus a bright-colored, flowered dress at the big store, W. P. Massuere Company. Had I been older, I might have cheered her on—and maybe I did say a kind, appreciative word, even at that young age of three. I did help her out in other ways if I saw the need. She deserved such good things, and it was good that she sometimes did do special things for herself. "Bless you, Mother!" is my cheer! And I anoint your spirit with my tears of love and thanks for all that you have done. We took the bus home, and that was a very special day. It was my first ride on the train and my first bus ride. "Ethel Mae seemed to enjoy it," she said in her low-keyed way to others, while inside my head, I was probably bursting with the experience of the train and entranced with the softly bouncing, swinging ride and the rhythmic sound of the metal wheels rolling on the metal tracks. So she was doing good things for me too.

For three months when I was three, we had a dog. Ben was working as the agent and telegrapher in Wisconsin Rapids in January, and he found a blue-gray puppy half-frozen on the snowy street near a tree in below-freezing weather. Ben picked him up and took the midnight freight train home to Whitehall with the now warmed-up puppy. The next day, Dallas received his new camera from Montgomery Ward and took pictures of me, several others, and the dog that Ben called "Poochie." He then left for another fill-in agent's job in *Luxemburg, Wisconsin,* settled by families from the Grand Duchy of Luxembourg in Europe, and left Poochie in our care. I was eager for the job. I held, talked to, and played with him, my mother said. He was my home entertainment. A week later, I brought the dog down in the basement where Mother was washing clothes. The dog bothered her while she was trying to work, so I said, "Never mind, I will take care of him," and I took him, "mad as he seemed," my mother said. So that was one of the ways I helped my mom. Those were joyous months, with the Christmas cactus blooming in the living room the first of February; Mother's fiftieth birthday to celebrate on the third with telegrams and neighbors; me measuring up on the depot scale at 3 feet, 1½ inches tall; a blizzard of snow on the twenty-eighth too deep to walk in but beautiful to see and play in and school still in session until noon for my brothers and sisters; Dad's fiftieth in March with angel food cake; walks in the cold evenings around the town with my parents and sometimes Leone with a friend or two; warm aromas of pumpkin pie, rolls, and cakes coming from the wood-fueled oven; and a puppy to love and bathe. But my parents had other ideas for the dog. Mother asked her sister Celia if her family wanted him, and they did not. Dad took Poochie to the depot later in March to inquire of Mr. Ackley from near Pigeon Falls what kind of a dog he was, as he was coming in to ship one of his shepherd dogs. He said Poochie was a rat terrier and would not be worth more than two or three dollars. On April Fools' Day, Agnes Lund from Northfield came to take Poochie home with her, no fooling, as my parents were giving it to her for free. I guess I took it all in stride; Mother did not say. It was a wonderful time, having a rescued, adopted, orphan puppy creature with a mutual love and caring devotion between us, but the time was over, and life went on.

I wasn't too young in my toddler years to hear about and be fascinated by special events that came to town or to the surrounding country. Mother and I went to an auction in the back of F. B. Olson's Hardware Store on a July morning in 1939. The Toftes were selling their household goods, and Mother, with her thrifty ways, bought a dishpan, cooking kettle, chopping bowls, and a rubber mat all for forty cents. The auctioneer was mesmerizing. How could he talk so rapidly in a musical tone and a jumble and stutter of words that people still seemed to understand, bidding a price back and forth with others until the auctioneer said, "Fourteen dollars. Is that the last bid? Going, going, gone, for fourteen dollars for that lucky buyer!" And then he would start again with another chair or mirror or box of books. Farm auctions were even more fascinating. All these strong, weathered men in overalls were bidding on farm equipment that to my eyes looked grand. Green John Deere machinery and red International Harvester tractors and imposing equipment of all varieties for tilling soil, planting seeds, clearing weeds, cutting down crops, and binding for bales of hay were spread out on the fields. Dad took me to the farm auctions just for his entertainment, I think, and certainly for mine.

My siblings entertained us too. The two younger boys of the four in our family, Sherman and Dallas, were passionate basketball players in high school. They traveled throughout Trempealeau County with their team, playing other high school teams, participating in tournaments, making the newspapers and radio broadcasts, and winning awards. But making even bigger news were the Harlem Globetrotters, who came to town when the boys were around fourteen and fifteen. The Globetrotters were called Negroes, and they played whatever team a city had to offer. On Friday, January 21, 1938, they played the Whitehall team in the Whitehall High School gymnasium. I was only two at the time and was at home asleep in my small bed, pushed against the wall and a couple of feet over from Ma's double bed in her bedroom. Sherman and Dallas had the fun of playing on the Whitehall team, but the Globetrotters won thirty-five to thirty-two. They had a reputation of entertaining with skillful, funny tricks and of keeping the score reasonably close and the excitement high. That was a rare occasion for the town to see black people, whom we read about in books.

The small town of Whitehall had the distinction of having a ski jump and a town full of boys eagerly taking up the sport. It was in good part thanks to my brothers. My oldest brother, Ben, in 1933 and 1934, organized The Record Breakers Ski Club to include Ben, Ray, Sherman, Dallas, and their friends. They, with the help of their dads, built a ski jump on Allen Hill, on the edge of the golf course behind our house. One fine Sunday, a crowd of fans collected to see the kids do their stuff. Ben and the boys had organized a tournament, and they put on an exhibition of ski jumping "that was long to be remembered in the annals of the sport," as my dad said. "The fans got more of a kick out of this than anything the adults had put on." After the tourney, the adults took up a collection and built the kids a larger ski hill and jump on Allen Hill with regular meets and tournaments.

I watched the daring feat of the ski-jumping spectacle with very young eyes and while very bundled up in snowy, freezing, windy weather. In the summer I climbed up and down the Allen Hill ski jump on the splinter-filled steps alongside the scaffold. At the top, standing on the platform, I would imagine myself skiing down a hard, snow-covered, angled track with a curve at the bottom leading to the takeoff and then sailing into the air and landing far below, like my brothers did. Just imagining that was daring enough for me.

There was another, bigger ski jump outside of town off County Road D in Thompson Coulee. My brothers and their buddies jumped in tournaments all over the county and beyond. Later, Ray was on the University of Wisconsin–Madison ski jumping team. Several of the Record Breakers became professional ski jumpers and entered the big meets. Banquets were held for all the skiers and the winners, as picked by a self-appointed adult judge who was knowledgeable in skiing. They won awards in different "letter classes" in the Whitehall Club House just a hill over from Allen Hill. But there were injuries. In one tournament in January 1941 in Thompson Coulee, three skiers got hurt. Gunner Imen had a severe concussion, Joe Nelson broke his leg in practice, and Harold Melzer broke his collarbone on the opening jump.

Having a ski jump was special, but it was also remarkable and chichi for this small town to have a clubhouse and golf course. The doctor brothers E. A. and R. L. McCornack, the dentist Dr. Anton Vold, and our neighbor Sig Hegge instigated the idea in the 1920s. They liked to golf and wanted a place to play their sport, get exercise, and socialize. So their talk led to action when Sig offered some of his acreage to make the course and fit a clubhouse in the center edge of the land. They purchased more land to have the course extended all the way from the Trempealeau River Bridge on the east end to the Lambersons' farm on the west. The beautiful, rolling fairways from tee to green, behind and beyond my house, served as my playground through all my growing-up years. The course offered a free time for kids to golf on early Saturday mornings before the grownups started teeing off and hills for tobogganing, sledding, and skiing in the glistening winter snow with a thermos of hot cocoa tucked into a bag, for picnicking with friends, and for roaming alone.

Another attraction for this town was the appearance of the tallest man in the world. Robert Pershing Wadlow and his dad parked their truck between Erickson's Store and Briggs Auto Sales on a Saturday afternoon in September 1939. My mother and my grandmother, with me in tow, saw him from 1:30 to 2:30 standing in the back of his truck. He was twenty-one years old and 8 feet 8¼ inches tall (perhaps an overactive pituitary, then untreatable), weighed 491 pounds, and wore shoes nineteen inches long, a size-nineteen shirt collar, and shoes weighing four pounds each, made by Peter's Shoe Company in St. Louis. His father, from England, was 5 feet 11¼" tall, and his mother, of average height, was Swedish, like my parents. Robert was advertising Peter's Shoes. He died not long after his Whitehall appearance of a foot abscess infection. Was it the heavyweight shoes?

There were other places to go and other things to learn, and my mother and I went hand-in-hand for visits to the Whitehall High School, which all my siblings attended. One building housed all the grades. The three-story, brown brick rectangle sat on a slight rise on a large green square of lawn edged by Dewey, Hobson, and Park Streets. Sometimes she needed to talk to a teacher or the principal, and I got to see the long, wide hall on the second floor with all the elementary classrooms. On the third floor was the high school, where two of my brothers, who were still at home, spent their days. The gym, home economics, and industrial arts rooms were on the basement/first-floor level. In May 1939, Avis, in seventh grade, brought an invitation home to visit her classroom the next day. So Mother and I went to see, in one classroom, the seventh and eighth grades. Avis was an excellent student, and she set an example for me in the coming years. On another day in the spring, mothers of second graders were asked to visit their classroom. I'm not sure if I was there on this occasion, but the children were asked to show and tell what their fathers did to help the country. Leone had drawn a picture of the depot and told the class that Daddy got up in the morning, went to the depot, delivered telegrams, and sent telegrams, and on Saturdays, her brother would go there and help Dad deliver telegrams and take care of the mail. Well, even if that was all he did (and it was not), Dad was serving his country well.

The elementary school kids all had their turns at being in whatever operetta was put on that year. Mother always sewed our costumes. She sewed the operetta dress and cap when Leone was in second grade out of white cheesecloth. Leone went to Hewett Pharmacy with five cents for Christmas snow to sprinkle on the absorbent cotton knob on the cap. I watched Mother sew that and many other dresses for herself and us girls, white cotton dress shirts for Dad with a special high collar to cover an abscess surgery scar on his neck that he was self-conscious about, and many quilts—"logging quilts" were her specialty—and repairs and alterations of anything made with fabric on her treadle Singer sewing machine. In the trusting, open household we had for allowing us independence at a very young age, I experimented on my own. I took sewing into my own hands at age three by sewing the needle right through the tip of my long finger on my left hand with the sewing machine. The needle broke off, leaving the metal imbedded in my flesh. Ma took me to Dr. Tyvand's residence. He told her to soak some absorbent cotton in Borax, wrap it around my finger, leave it for two or three days, and come see him again. The needle, he said, could then be removed by squeezing the finger. After three days, my dad took it out with the knife he always kept in his pocket. It hurt, and I cried hard. My father fastened the broken needle to a page in my baby book. I was not deterred by needles and learned to sew by hand before I was old enough for school. I made patterns for doll clothes out of newspaper and cut them out of my mother's fabric remnants for my neighbor friends Audrey, Clarice, and Patty and for me, and then we sewed them as we sat on a blanket in my front yard. Learning to sew so young was a skill that my sisters and I have used and perfected throughout our lives, thanks to my mother's teaching us by example.

Like the threading in her quilts—that firm, continuous network holding the fabric pieces together—church was the core of our family's days and weeks and years. It permeated and manifested itself in all our activities, especially music for me. Barely three, I burst into song at home while my Mother listened:

In my heart, there rings a melody,
There rings a melody with heaven's harmony.
In my heart there rings a melody,
There rings a melody of love!

The hymn was so beautiful and uplifting, and I radiated the message for decades to come. It was a common occurrence for all of us to go to services at any one of the churches in town: the Pentecostal Tabernacle and the First Baptist, First Methodist, and Our Savior's Lutheran Churches. One Sunday when I was four, Avis went to the Baptist Church while the rest of us attended the Methodist one, and in the evening, Sherman and Avis went to the Lutheran Church to be an usher and a singer in a choir gown, respectively. The attorney in town, Mr. O. J. Eggum, took Dallas, and Mr. Hinkle, the high school band director, took Sherman to the Fathers and Sons Banquet at the Lutheran church. And in turn, even the daughters of Rev. Birkeland of the Lutheran Church came to the Baptist church for special services. The Catholics went to Saints Peter and Paul Catholic Churches in Independence, and when I entered high school, they built a church on the hill on the southern outskirts of Whitehall. It was ecumenism manifest, with Dad, by the time I came along, questioning all theology and thinking of God not as a personal God but as the first cause of everything and rarely attending church, and Mother taking a literal translation of the Bible to heart. Together they added up to an ecumenical testimony to beliefs and ethics and morals. As I had hummed another hymn on my return visit to Whitehall in 2008, "How Firm A Foundation," the church experience lasted throughout our growing-up years and for all our lives to come.

Arvid and Sarah's Courtship

MY PARENTS GREW OUT of similar roots. Their families' nationality, religion, education, economic status, hardship, and place of birth could have all been one and the same.

My dad's parents, Karren Olson Erickson and Nels Olaf Erickson, were born in Sundsvall, Sweden, in 1852 and 1851, respectively, were married in Sundsvall, and within four years lost their first four infants, Ellen Elenore, Carl William, Erik, and Ellen, to diphtheria, all of whom they buried in Sweden. Then Nels and Karren emigrated by ship on separate trips to the United States in 1880 and 1881, respectively, to start a new life and family.

Karren, twenty-seven and not speaking English, traveled alone by ship, by boat, and by foot, carrying her luggage to Muskegon, Michigan, where she was to meet her husband. She only knew that he was working in a sawmill. An emigrant family directed her to a large, two- or three-story boarding house on a lake. She wasn't sure of finding him there, but she took a room for the night on the top story. The place was primitive, and the men were rough-and-tumble, but she had no fear. Though she was a gentle spirit, she could be tough when needed. Resting in her room on that early evening in the summer of 1881, she wondered what to do next to find her husband. The workers had finished their workday and were lounging in front of their boarding house. She opened her window and leaned out to see the men more easily. She saw a row of legs of men leaning against the building, but their owners were not visible to her. She stared at the knitted socks on the legs stretched out on the ground. Being an expert knitter, she readily recognized the different types of knitting done on the socks. As her eyes ran along the row of feet and legs, there was one pair of long legs and feet whose socks looked familiar. The type of knitting was exactly like her own that she had made into socks and sent to her husband while she was still in Sweden. "Is it possible," she asked herself, "that these socks were knitted by me? They certainly look like those I knitted." Excited now, she decided to take a chance. "Nils, Nils," she screamed. There was a flurry of excitement among the men below, when they saw a good-looking young woman leaning out the window and attracting their attention. Women were scarce in that part of the world those days, and men would fight over available girls. She called his name again. Finally my grandfather realized that it was his name being called and that the voice was familiar. He unwound his long legs, got to his feet (for it really was Nils), and stretched to his full 6 feet 2 inches. When he looked up at the window, he knew at once she was his wife, Karren. They ran to meet inside the building, and a happy moment for both ensued.

Ready to face the future together, they settled in Jackson County, Wisconsin. Nels (Nils), a lumberjack, eventually built a log cabin in Oak Ridge, in which they raised their new, growing family of nine children, making for Karren's strong, resilient body and psyche a total of thirteen offspring, including the infants who were born and died in Sweden. In addition to Nels's work in the sawmill, he and Karren farmed their land with crops and milk cows. Arvid, my father-to-be, the sixth in line of the nine, was born in the small mill settlement of Goodyear in the "Big Swamp" that had been a glacial lake at the end of the last ice age, fifteen to nineteen thousand years ago. "Glacial Lake Wisconsin" dried up enough to become seeded in some mysterious way by white, Norway, and Jackson pine trees. The names of Nels and Karren's nine children—five boys and four girls, including two sets of twins—born in the United States were written down in records in the Lutheran Church. In order of birth, they were Anna May, twins Alfred and Alfreda, twins Albert and Albion, Arvid, Mamie, Harry, and Martha. Later, Karren and the children became Baptist. But both Karren's clay-pipe-smoking, whiskey-flask-in-her-hip-pocket mother Kerstin Christina Stais Andersdotter Larson Olson, who lived to eighty-nine years and died of old age, and Karren's husband, Nels, were independent thinkers and skeptical of all religions. Kerstin thought that the Bible was a very controversial book that did not settle anything. But my dad said that his Grandma Olson's heart was of gold. Nels, Arvid's father, never attended church. He had no interest in church creeds or dogmas and didn't interfere with those who did, including his wife, Karren. My dad called his mother and father practical Christians, practicing Christian ethics in their daily lives. The children all had limited schooling in small schoolhouses and were self-taught to read and write. Their religious training took place at home with their own reading of the Bible, with traveling preachers until church buildings were built, and at occasional church tent meetings. Music filled all the spaces. Karren had a beautiful singing voice and sang solos and duets in church and in the town hall. Two of their five boys, Arvid, my dad, and Albert took up the mandolin and the guitar and played for dances. (Dad kept his mandolin, played it when I was a preschooler, and then pretty much stopped.)

My mother's parents, Blom Olaf Larson and Sarah Erickson Larson, were born in Dala Jarna, Sweden, in 1855 and 1862, respectively. Their families knew each other in that small town. When Sarah Erickson (same as my mother's married name) was a teenager in Sweden, she and her parents came on a ship to the United States. She brought all that she needed to set up a household: linens, pots and pans, a spinning wheel, and a loom for weaving rugs that, seventy years later, I saw and sat at in my youth. Blom Olaf came by himself on a ship to America after Sarah arrived. Blom Olaf and Sarah, thirty and twenty-three, respectively, were married in Merrillan, Wisconsin, in 1885. They helped start the Baptist Church in the country, called Garden Valley, where they cleared virgin timber and moved rock to make a farm, raising crops and milk cows. My mother to be, Sarah Larson, was the fourth child out of nine children, eight girls and one boy. A tenth child, number seven in order of birth and a twin to the sixth child, did not survive. Schooling took place at a little white schoolhouse around the bend from their farm.

The Ericksons, on my dad's side, and the Larsons, on my mother's side, both lived on country farms about thirty miles apart. Karren used to journey to Garden Valley for companionship among the Swedes and to attend Baptist religious services, and she knew Blom Olaf and Sarah well. But Sarah and Arvid, my parents, did not meet until they were working for their own keep.

After elementary school, Sarah continued to help out on the farm, and she also worked as a waitress and as a chambermaid at the Hotel Campbell in Merrillan, Wisconsin. When Sarah was twenty-four, Mrs. Cannon wrote to her on December 30, 1913, that "I am depending on your coming back to work for me and hope you won't disappoint me as I need you. Your work has been very satisfactory here and I would like you to start work right after New Year's as soon as you can."

When Arvid was around fifteen, he looked for jobs to earn some cash, and from then on, he never asked his parents for money. He searched for empty beer, whisky, and brandy bottles to sell to the saloon bartender for five or ten cents each. The bottles were then refilled from barrels of beer and liquor to sell. He worked for a grocery store by hitching a horse to a delivery wagon to take orders and deliver groceries. He planed boards in a refrigerator company and cut off the end of his little finger on his left hand (ever after, he hid that finger under his ring finger). In the winter, he worked for an ice company, harvesting ice for home iceboxes from a frozen lake. Then he attended high school in Rhinelander, playing hooky and loafing around the Soo Line Railroad switchyards, where his love of trains took hold, starting when he was five in Oak Ridge. In the telegraph office, he listened to the "music of the telegraph key" and searched out a telegraph school. He bought a train ticket to Eau Claire and enrolled in the Northwestern Telegraph School on Barstow Street. Arvid paid Mr. L. P. Loken, the owner and teacher, one hundred dollars to cover tuition and a room, almost a fortune in those days. The money and the teaching lasted three months, and he was then ready for a job in St. Paul. That was in July 1909. He moved around to several railroad stations in Minnesota and Texas and then back to various towns in Wisconsin. It was at his Woodville "trick" that his health started to fail and he was operated on for swollen, infected glands on both sides of his neck. This left him with scars, a very weak, listless body, and a disheartened spirit. Thus began his interest in the diet, fasting, and exercise plan of well-known health advocate, Bernarr McFadden, to slowly regain his health.

He longed for a home and a family. His wellbeing was still shaky, and he wanted someone to care for him in illness, to wish to share his fortunes and misfortunes, and to be a homemaker and a loving companion.

And then Arvid met Sarah. He was on his way to his folks' home when he stopped to change trains in Merrillan, where Sarah was serving tables in the lunchroom of the Campbell Hotel. Arvid's sister Martha, who happened to be there at the time, introduced Arvid to Miss Sarah Larson. Sarah welcomed him and encouraged him to call when he could. They were both twenty-five and professed the same religion. He saw that she had a good reputation and was a good manager of financial affairs. Sarah was of such a calm, caring nature that Arvid felt right at home with her, and they began to see each other and write letters. They held hands while they strolled the country lanes. They talked about their yearnings. Sarah took Arvid home to meet her parents on the farm. In the course of time, he asked her if she would take him, such as he was, for better or worse, as a life partner.

On July 20, 1914, from his "trick" at Woodville, Arvid wrote a six-page letter to Sarah.

Dear Sarah - I received your very nice letter OK and was very glad to get it. Am rather slow about answering this time, as I had a tooth ache all day Saturday, but am all right now. Had it fixed yesterday. Sunday I worked nearly all day. Had fine services in church last night. Wish you had been here. Mrs. Moe says 'Why don't you bring her here and settle down.' I didn't answer her anything. She says to tell you hello. Did you hear about a man being killed on track near Fall Creek today. I just heard over the wire that some train run over a man by name of Herman Konke from Alma Center, this A.M. Do you know him? Am very anxious to see you as I have a lot to talk about. It's easier to talk 'by hand' you know than by U.S. mail. But if I can get away, I'll see you August 1st. If I can't get away then, will try August 8th. Will let you know. The farmers around here are still very busy making hay. Am wishing I had a hand in it. I'll have a farm someday if all goes well. If you should decide to marry me, which I am hoping you will, I would try to rent a small place a little ways in country, if I could possibly, to start with. I would rather live on a farm than in a town. Have always preferred a farm, but as long as a person is single it's pretty hard to get a farm paid for. Say, that insurance I carry, comes due next month, the 3rd, and if I knew for sure, that I was going to drop it, I would 'ent pay them any more on it. If I were to have my way about it, I would keep it up, now, that I had started with it and not lose the money. But if I knew that you would be my wife, some day, and you are against it, I would be glad to drop it. To tell the truth It's a graft in a way. But it's a good thing for a single man who has nothing and hard for him to save money. Am going to try to get some of my money back. I wish I knew what you are going to do about it. If you refuse me, I don't think I'll ever marry. If there is anything I can do to help you decide just tell me. I must close now and get to work. Pls write soon. God be with you. With Love, Your Friend, Arvid

Two days later, on July 22, 1914, Sarah wrote a four-page letter on Hotel Campbell Railroad Eating House stationary.

Dear Arvid, Received your most welcome letter yesterday and also one today. Am very glad every time they say it's mail for me. Hoping it is from you, which it most always is. Unless I get a letter from my folks. Got a letter from my Mother this a.m. She is planning on coming home the 1st Aug. About that place Mrs Moe spoke to you about. Would be nice in a way to work around there, so I could see you more often. But as long as I am used to this place, I think I'd better stick to it, awhile yet anyway. What I don't like is to change about with places. So don't think I'll ever come to Woodvill and work. Unless I would come and work for you. But must tell you, I am a poor cook. Is nice of Mrs. Moe to think of me, And try her best to get me a place. Would write to her. But have not got her box no. Please tell her hello for me. Well: Arvid, It seems such a long time since you was here. Is very lonesome around here without you. Would be very glad to see you again and have a good talk with you. Seem such a long time to wait until the First or Eight of Aug. My Father have not went to Centuria yet. But think he will go the last of this week, if he is going at all. Don't spose you'll care about going out there unless he is home. I think he will be back the First thou. So if you come that day you'll take the same train I s'pose No 16. Have not heard anything about the man that got killed, until I got your letter yesterday A.M. Yesterday P.M. Ruth took the train to Alma Center. She been having the toothache for a few days. So went over there and got her tooth pulled. She had a ride back with a fellow that use to be a neighbor to us. But is now married and lives in the town of Alma Center. He was telling Ruth about this Herman Domkey being run over by some train near Fall Creek. He was one of our neighbors down home. A German. We been having pretty dry and hot weather now days. Good for haying. See you prefer a farm which I do also. No place like the country for me. Of course I wouldn't mind living in town for a while. Last Sat. Ruth & I walked to Alma Center and back again, excepting we had a car ride about ½ mile. We had our pictures taken. I had mine taken on postals. Got the proofs yesterday. Last Sun. PM. Hannah and I was to church at N. Mattsons. In the eve I went to bed at 8. Mon PM Hannah, Ruth & I was out picking raspberries. We did not have any bonnets, so made some out of newspaper. You just ought to have seen us. Ruth and I picked four qts together. We canned them at Grandpas made 3 qts of sauce. Been talking about going some other day, but pretty hard to get time, having to do our washing and ironing on spare time. I washed yesterday PM and ironed in the eve until 8. Went to bed at 9. I ought to do some sewing too but don't feel like doing more than what I have to these hot days. Look so we are going to have some rain tonite, which I hope we will. See that insurance comes due next month the 3rd you say you'd be glad to drop it. If you'd be sure I'd be your wife some day, and I was against it. I really would feel bad to see you loose all, or most of that money, that you been working so hard for. But if I should marry you I know I wouldn't feel happy with you if you'd carry the insurance. If you should drop it, I hope you won't be reminding me of that money you had to loose for my sake. Because that would make me feel very bad. Hope I can see you soon, If not before I hope you can surely come the 1st Aug. Must say goodnite. Please write soon. God be with you. I am your Friend Sarah

Early in August, during Arvid and Sarah's times together, strolling the country lanes, and in letters unseen by me that did not survive the decades, Sarah agreed that she would take Arvid, such as he was, for better or worse, as a life partner. And she would try to do the best she knew how for him, and he for her. They planned to marry later in the year.

On a hot day in the middle of August, Arvid set out for a new "trick" in Hustler from Woodville in good spirits. His hours were 7:00 a.m. to 7:00 p.m., seven days a week. In addition to telegraph and station work, his duties were to care for the two switch lights, carry the US mail between the depot and the post office for the passenger trains; keep burning the train order signal light, the kerosene lamps in office and waiting room, and all other lights using kerosene; and keeping the waiting and office floors spick and span. He found Hustler to be nice and pleasant, and he was proud of his station and tried hard to please his employers. On the personal front, with Sarah agreeing to marriage, he said, "I had a renewed hope, a stronger faith in the future, regardless of my sickness and the war clouds that hung over Europe."

On October 20, 1914, Sarah wrote from Alma Center,

My Dear Arvid, Will try and be at Merrillan next Sun. Ruth is coming home I guess, so can go down there when they take her back. Think I can finish my quilts this week so may stop at Merrillan and work for 2 or 3 weeks if I can get Mrs Larson to sew my dress for me. Will write to my Sisters and tell them to go over there and ask her. Hope you can come Sun. as I got so much to talk to you about. Say Arvid do you have to belong to a Union to keep that job, have not thought much about it when you did not say anything about it when I told you long time ago that I didn't believe in either Unions or Lodges. Hope you don't belong to it. Pa said yesterday he thought all the railroad men had to belong to the Union. Wish you had been here last nite so I could have talked to you. Felt so down hearted to think about that. And then Pa, Ma and Anna was quarelling all eve. Feel so bad to hear so much quarreling. Can't help but cry sometime. Cryed all last nite and also started in this morning again. Hope that you and I will always live peacefully together. May we always have Jesus as our best friend. Life here on Earth is short, may we therefore strive to reach a better place. I long O I long to be there. Pray for me Hope to hear from you soon and tell me if you can be in Merrilan Sun. Would like so much to see my dear Arvid again. I think of you often. Your with Love Sarah –

With a prompt receipt of her letter the same day that she wrote it and mailed it, Arvid wrote back on the twentieth, and it was postmarked on the twenty-first.

My Dear Little Girl – I received your long letter yesterday and another short one today. I did'ent expect to get one today, but its very good to hear from you. Keep the good work up. Am sorry to hear that you have to listen to so much quarreling. But don't let that bother you. Just let them quarrel and don't pay any attention. Of course its bad to have to hear such things, but just flee to Jesus for comfort. He is always your best friend in sorrow or joy. We have nothing to fear if he is our friend. Would like to be with you awful bad, but I'll see you next Sunday night at Merrillan if it's God's will and nothing happens to prevent it. You spoke about me belonging to a union. I do belong to the Order of Railroad Telegraphers, but I don't intend to keep it paid up. I have dropped out of it several times then paid up again. I don't have to belong to it unless I want to and I can get a job and keep it as long as I want to without belonging to any order. It costs 10 dollars a year to belong to it. I am going to drop it, so don't let that bother you any. We will talk about it when I see you Sunday night. I have been thinking lately, about farming. The more I think of it the better it looks to me. I think that will be the only way to get anything ahead. We will talk about it when I see you. I am going to pick out the wedding rings tonight. Suppose I better get about 18 or 22 Karet price about 6 or 7 dollars. Will that be all right? I'll get them both alike. I wrote to Rev Klein asking him to perform the ceremony. He answered and said he would hold Nov 21 open, and that he was glad I asked him so long ahead of time, as he has engagements to fill many days in advance. He wants to know how he will get out there. If he should hire a livery or if some one will come and get him. How about that? Can you get to B.R.Falls and get that license before you go back to work, or any time between now and Nov 4th. I must get to bed now. Will let you know how many invitations I'll need. If you have them along with you to Merrillan. I'll take what I need then. Happy Dreams. God be with you till we meet again. Love to my Dear Sarah. We will make up for lost time next Sunday night if I can get away, which I will manage some way. Lovingly Yours Arvid

Arvid rented a house in Hustler with a bachelor friend, James Freeborn, who ran a patent medicine and delicatessen store in town, for the "huge sum," as Arvid said years later in his autobiography, of seven dollars per month. Jamie agreed when they rented the house together that he would leave when Arvid was to occupy it with his wife soon after their marriage. One day, a big wooden box came for Arvid by freight from Merrillan. It contained the "hope chest" of his wife-to-be. When he opened it and saw all those women's clothes and articles, it gave him a strange feeling. It cast a sort of "spell" over him, he said. He asked for job "relief" for the Thanksgiving period. Sarah and Arvid had set the wedding date for the day following Thanksgiving, November 21, 1914.

Thinking that the stabilizing influence of the church and its moral teachings would be beneficial to him and his future family, Arvid joined the Baptist chapel in his community, the church to which his mother had belonged. He said,

I did that as a free agent because I felt I should belong to an organization of that sort, more for security and consolation than for any other reason. I did not feel the need for a so called 'salvation;' I could not see what I should be "saved" from; I was not a criminal or a law breaker, and I had been trying to live a good life as much as I could; I did not feel guilty of anything. I did not think that "salvation" consisted of being "saved" from an eternal punishment that was said to be the case if we did not accept it literally as they said it. I thought that would be altogether too drastic for a mere belief or a non-belief. Rather salvation would be a gradual and steady process of improvement of one's self; advancement in morals; in ethics; spiritual awareness of a Supreme Being with Divine Justice; progress towards betterment in intellect, good thinking. That is the only "salvation" worth while, because by so doing we save ourselves from the consequences of our own follies.

Formal invitations, 5" x 6½", printed on vellum, were sent out, with one-cent stamps on the envelopes.

Mr. and Mrs. B. O. Larson
request the honor of your presence
at the marriage of their daughter
Sarah
to
Arvid Erickson

Saturday afternoon
November twenty-first
Nineteen Hundred Fourteen
at three o'clock
at their home in Garden Valley, Wisconsin

Everything was set for the wedding. Rev. A. R. Klien, the Methodist minister from Merrillan, was to officiate. The ceremony took place in the bride's parents' home on the farm. Guests, relatives, and friends filled the house to see the composed and lovely dark-haired bride and her handsome mate joined in marriage. Sarah, a fine seamstress, with possible help from Mrs. Larson, was adorned in her own design: a white, hand-made, fine-cotton, floor-length gown, with layers of lace and a fitted waist. Arvid wore a dark suit and a white high-collared shirt with a white bow tie. Both wore white carnations, he on his lapel, she in her hair, which was loosely pulled back in a bun. She held a cascade of white carnations with her left hand, her other hand in her new husband's. After the ceremony, a bountiful repast was served in the evening for all present. It was late when the last guest had departed. Arvid and Sarah remained in the house for the night, and the next day they left for Black River Falls by train from Alma Center, someone taking them in a horse and buggy to the depot for picture taking by Mr. A. J. Roisland. That evening, they boarded a train from Black River Falls to Chicago, having reserved a Pullman berth. "Thus a new phase of life was begun as others had before us," Arvid wrote, "an experience as old as humanity itself, a response to Nature's call to mate." And he caught the moment with a poem.

Beloved bride and bridegroom may
Your wedding day be bright,
And may the light of silver stars,
Adorn your wedding night
There will be disappointments and
There will be little tears,
But they will serve to strengthen you,
Throughout the married years

After their honeymoon in Chicago, my parents arrived in Hustler to begin housekeeping in the Steele House. As soon as word got around that a newly married couple had arrived in the house, a crowd of people assembled in front of it after dark and put on a chivaree with noise-making gadgets. They whooped it up until Arvid came out and gave them some money with which to buy cigars and drinks. Arvid resumed his work at the depot, and he and Sarah got down to the business of living a married life.

Their quiet, steady union continued for fifty-seven more years until their deaths just over a year apart in 1971 and 1973, respectively, Arvid at 82 and Sarah at 83. They weren't showy with their love. My sister remembers trying to open the stairwell door and finding Mother's hand holding the doorknob to not let anyone in, while Leone caught a glimpse of Mother kissing Dad sweetly at the bottom of the stairs. They loved, respected, and honored each other for their commitment to share a lifetime on this earth. And as Sarah had wished when they courted, they had peace in their marriage. Special days were remembered and celebrated usually in simple ways. An anniversary was a time for stuffed pork chops and angel food cake. For their twenty-fifth, silver wedding anniversary, they wrote several radio stations in Eau Claire, Stevens Point, La Crosse, and Minneapolis, to have their day and names announced on the air and songs sung in their honor on November 21, 1939. Telegrams and cards came from friends, and photos were taken of them with Mother still fitting into her wedding dress of twenty-five years ago. A carnation was in her hair, and Dad wore one on his lapel, just like on their wedding day. Valentines were exchanged throughout their years. After twenty-seven years of marriage, Arvid gave Sarah a valentine, which summed up their years of caring for each other.

Valentine Greetings
To My Wife
Our own friendly home
from its floor to its beams.
With its own little style,
is my castle of dreams.
And the one thing
that makes it so
cherished and fair
Is the love of the girl
who is waiting me there.
A-

O! Segari!

My MOTHER'S PARENTS CAME to America on a boat from Sweden in 1880. Like most emigrants from the old land, they wanted less hardship and a better life. Blom Olaf and Sarah Larson heard about the freedoms and opportunities in the new land. So they made their way by boat across the Atlantic and by foot and boat through the Saint Lawrence Seaway to the rich, open land in Wisconsin. They found rolling farmland much like what they had had in Sweden and settled in Jackson County, abundant in White Pine. People who immigrated mostly lumbered and farmed, and Blom Olaf and Sarah found acreage for cows and crops in Garden Valley. That's where my mother was born.

Sarah, my grandmother, was pregnant much of her fertile life, as was common among early settlers. Birth control, if it was used at all, was not very effective. There were miscarriages and infant deaths along the way. It was nature's way, without the assistance of hygiene and modern medical practices. The children who survived were expected from a young age on to help with the household chores, watch after the younger children, do heavy farm work in the fields, and milk the cows.

Sarah, small but strong, produced nine girls and one boy who survived past infancy. In order of birth, she named them Anna, Emma, Marie, Sarah (my mother), Ruth, Esther, Lydia (with a twin, Ellen, who died at birth because the midwife didn't see her and cut the cord too soon), William, Ellen (using the name again), and Celia. It was special for Sarah, fourth in line, to be named after her mother, as well as her grandmother, Sarah Persdotter Jacobson, in Sweden.

All ten grew into adulthood on the farm. They walked to a white, one-room schoolhouse with a small bell tower around the bend along a rutty gravel road. They spoke English in school but Swedish at home.

After my mother was married and had her own passel of seven kids, with me bringing up the rear, we drove to Garden Valley often. The now-grownups almost all stayed close to their childhood home. I knew them all.

My uncle Willie was in my life the least. The one boy in my mother's family fathered five boys of his own, as if to get a break from all the girls he grew up with or to make up for any male deprivation in his life. It was my aunts who intrigued me.

We made the rounds of the sisters' farms. Dad drove us in our 1934 black Ford four-door sedan, bought new for less than one thousand dollars cash from their savings and a rare purchase during the Great Depression, but Dad had a steady salary with the railroad. Years later, we replaced it with a 1938 green Ford sedan, and then a green Pontiac. Four or five of us could fit in the back of either Ford sedan, with someone holding me on their lap and one or two squeezed on the bench seat in the front between our parents. There was hardly another car on the road. In almost any weather, the dirt roads were rough "washboards" and deep ruts. Tires went flat easily, and Dad fixed them with a repair kit. At least once we got stuck in mud, and a man with a team of horses nearby pulled us out. We had no windshield wipers or heater and no gauges for speed or distance. The car was open to the wind and rain until wooden slides were installed to keep out the bad weather. But we were a lucky few to even have a car, and it was a handsome one.

My mother would ask us in the car, taking a democratic vote, where we wanted to have lunch and where to go for eats and dessert later in the afternoon. We usually voted for Aunt Esther's house for lunch—she was a good cook—and later to Aunt Lydia and Andrew's for cold cuts, homemade bread and butter, and dessert. The smooth, warm butter she made with cream in a butter churn by pushing a plunger up and down in a wooden barrel. And she baked good pie.

Esther Hanson and her dozen children—well, thirteen if you counted the 2½-year-old boy, David, who, like my older brothers, died young (Wayne Douglas at fourteen months died of pneumonia, with no antibiotics then, and Hilman Neal died at three weeks)—would welcome us in the late morning, even if they didn't know we were coming, and Esther would give us a little squeeze with her open arms. She cooked up a storm. She killed a chicken or two from the coop to bake and make gravy, got potatoes from the downstairs cellar to cook and mash with milk and butter, steamed whatever vegetables were in season or opened a glass quart jar of home-canned vegetables, and then got help to load up the large, heavy oak dining room table. Cool water, pumped from the windmill next to the house, filled our glasses.

Her husband Edward, thin in his bib overalls and looking worn out, took a break from his dairy farm chores. He gave a quiet prayer of thanks for the blessings, and we savored our meal.

When we piled into the car to leave, Esther stood there in her white cotton dress belted at the waist with small, yellow-and-blue-flower print and a white, pointed collar and cuffs below the shoulders. Tan, cotton-knit stockings twisted into a knot at midthigh modestly covered her legs (and supported the varicose veins from all her pregnancies), whatever the weather. Her children were scattered, and she stood alone on the gravel driveway outside our car windows. With us as a captive audience, she gave us a sermon. I was mesmerized with how she carried on.

"Are you saved? That's the important thing. You must believe in our heavenly father and his son Jesus, who died on the cross for our sins in order to set us free. You have to ask him for forgiveness for your sins in order to go to heaven. The blood of the lamb was shed for you. If you haven't asked for his forgiveness, you need to do it. We don't want to go to eternal fire, do we? Just pray to Jesus, right now."

We listened patiently for many minutes until she wound down her message. We waved goodbye as Dad pulled out of the driveway.

"Esther needs to stop preaching to us," Dad said with an edge of anger in his voice. "She forces herself on us, and I don't like it. That is what she sees as the doctrines and dogmas of the Bible. It's her interpretation. She thinks we are all going to hell, and we are not. She cannot impose her beliefs on us. We are free-thinking individuals, and we can make our own decisions. Her religion may help her to be good, but I don't want it."

My dad always impressed me more than any preaching we got from Esther or the church or anyone. At age five, I was beginning to sort out the requirements of the Baptist theology and practice. In August '41, walking home from the Baptist Church after hearing the Libby Family Orchestra, I asked "Ma, how is it those people wear such long dresses [the Libby Family]?" Ma said, "I suppose they feel so Jesus wants them to dress that way." Then I said, "Will Jesus let us wear the other?"

But, from the moment I could comprehend religious beliefs, I was of like mind with my Dad: we shape our own beliefs based on our own searching for what seems to make most sense to us, and no one can force us to believe their way. With the biblical threat of fire and damnation, Esther passed on her strong religious beliefs to her children. Four boys of Esther's twelve kids became ministers of the Assembly of God Church, and two girls married ministers. The remaining six stayed in the church throughout their lives.

Lydia did not preach at all. Dad drove for a few minutes through the valley. We passed the Garden Valley Cemetery, where my grandfather Blom Olaf and grandmother Sarah (when I was nine) were buried, to get to Uncle Andrew and Aunt Lydia's small dairy and chicken farm (with a couple of pigs) at the base of rolling hills, where we spent the rest of the afternoon.

Lydia and Andrew had no children. They loved children—they thoughtfully sent us valentines—and would have wanted kids, we think, but it didn't happen. She was thirty-nine when she married Andrew, who was three years younger than she was. Some family members had heard her say that she wished she had a daughter. Lydia was always a little sickly. People wondered how fertile she was and whether something happened to her at her birth when her twin sister Ellen died.

They came out onto the open porch of their white, one-story, shed-roofed, clapboard farmhouse when they saw us pull in the driveway. Lydia Larson Erickson, not large or tall, her ash-brown hair pulled back in a bun, was dressed in a green-printed, short-sleeved dress, belted at her somewhat full waist, with a V-neck collar trimmed in lace. Andrew was in his usual blue-cotton, long-sleeved, buttoned shirt and dark blue denim bib overalls. Sweet chuckles and soft smiles radiated from them to us as we climbed the three wooden steps to their open porch. Andrew Erickson held Lydia's arm gently as they looked at us and then into each other's twinkling eyes, sweetly and playfully. They were so naturally and simply in love. It was no wonder we loved them.

"O! Segari!" they exclaimed in Swedish. "Oh my!" Looking around at us and bending down to the smaller ones like me, they gave us a soft touch on the head or arm. "Hello. How was your trip? Esther said you would be on your way here."

We kids spotted the hoped-for lemon meringue pie cooling off in its glass pie-plate on the floor of the porch.

Lydia knew how to make pie succulent to our taste as well as to our eye with a flaky crust made of lard. The meringue was heaped just right, with a light brown, wavy burn spread across the top and browned in her wood-fed oven. Before a forkful even made it to your mouth, you could almost taste the lemon rind that she grated and folded so skillfully into the golden yellow custard, made on top of her stove. But eating it would come later.

I headed for her pump organ. My mother bought that organ for herself many years before and then gave it to Lydia. Sarah thought that everyone should have music in his or her house. It was in pristine condition and looking grand in Lydia's cozy living room. I opened the black hymnbook and played. My legs and toes were stretched out to pump the pedals, and I held the keys down with my fingers to keep the sound coming. Lydia loved to watch and hear me play. She sang along, her throat cords showing and her small mouth tautly rounded and I sang too.

All hail the power of Jesus's name!
Let angels prostrate fall,
Bring forth the royal diadem,
And Crown him Lord of all.

I loved the majesty of the music and the words, and I played and held each chord to feel the power. I sang the words and phrases like I knew what they meant—"prostrate" and "diadem" made their way into my lexicon, along with "ransomed from the fall" in the second verse. "Terrestrial ball" opened up my brain to new literary phrasing that was, from my first mouthing of "mamma" on the same evening that I stretched out my hands for Mother to take me in her arms at five months, so fascinated with words.

If a song had four or more sharps in it, I often transposed it to flats, which I could play with greater ease. Or I played a song in the written key and then transposed it to any key, so there wasn't too high a strain on Lydia's voice. I flipped the page to another hymn that I knew Lydia would like. I had so many songs I wanted to play.

Abide With Me; fast falls the eventide.
The darkness deepens; Lord with me abide.
When other helpers fail and comforts flee,
Help of the helpless, O abide with me.

There was a comfort in the words, even if I didn't believe some of it. Who cannot feel good knowing that someone cares about them?

When I was barely old enough for school at age four, I sat at the brown upright piano in Sarah and Blom Olaf's old homestead. Blom Olaf died before Leone and I were born, but Sarah was alive until I turned nine. After Sarah passed on, three of my single aunts continued to live there. Anna, Emma, and Ruth gave me a few clues about the piano and music, though they didn't play much if at all, and I was on my own to figure it out. I learned easily to read the music. Playing by ear and singing from my heart came naturally. With that as groundwork, I took to Lydia's pump organ with pleasure.

Enough songs were sung, and there were more things to do. Lydia started setting up her small wooden table in the kitchen. There was no dining room in this house. And I ran outside to explore with my siblings. The red barn was empty, except for the feeder calves at one end, a couple of kitties to catch the mice, and chattering sparrows, flying in and out of the high windows open at both ends of the hayloft. In the late afternoon, the cows would amble in from the pasture where they were grazing on nutrient-dense alfalfa, clover, and oat grass. We could see a half-mile up on the distant hill, the black and white Holstein cows, from the Holstein region in northern Germany. The Hansons, where we had just had lunch, had brown and white Guernseys, which originated from the island of Guernsey off the southern coast of Great Britain. We all came from somewhere else on this terrestrial ball, it seemed. You could smell the hay and manure from the barn and hear the sounds of mooing and lowing as the cows sauntered from that far pasture to one near the barn. They knew that relieving the weight of their bulging udders was not far off. Andrew did the milking mostly alone or sometimes with his brothers, Alfred and Emil, who lived nearby, or with Lydia's help, twice a day, at five, six, or seven o'clock in the morning and five, six or seven o'clock in the evening.

Some of that warm, sweet milk went into our glasses and in cottage cheese that Lydia had made earlier in the morning for our late-afternoon meal. Eggs from the small chicken coop had gone into that still-warm lemon meringue pie. The yolks had been stirred briskly into the filling, and the whites made up the meringue. How perfect to use all that was fresh and fragrant and just outside your door.

We all sat down in our straight-back, wooden chairs, passed down from Andrew's parents, and Lydia said grace. "Thank you, Lord, for bringing Arvid and Sarah and their children here safely. Thank you for this food, and bless us, we pray. In Jesus's name. Amen."

Andrew and Lydia passed around platters of sliced meat, cheese, and homemade white bread and butter, and then bowls of cottage cheese and sliced cucumbers. We ate politely and mostly quietly while the adults spoke about the cows giving good milk and the neighbors helping with the haying and how maybe we could've used some rain. With a little chuckling, they would say, "So you don't have to milk cows at home, do you? But you help around the house, don't you!" And we nodded our heads and said, "Yes. And we play with our friends, and we read." "That's good that you read," they agreed. "You all are smart and are good students. You will do well for yourselves when you grow up. Sarah and Arvid do a good job of raising you." We nodded our heads in assent. "And here is the lemon meringue pie," Lydia announced with a cute little smile.

We relished every bite. The lard crust was so delicately flaky and the filling, topped with frothy amber peaks, was so gloriously, deliciously smooth and tartly sweet. We all chimed in to thank Aunt Lydia and Uncle Andrew for the supper and the good pie as we rose from the table.

We left the Ericksons' sweet abode with the sun still hanging in the sky.

If we had time, we stopped to see Aunt Celia and Uncle Aaron and their four children on their chicken and dairy farm. They were just a half-mile up the road from Lydia's on our way home to Whitehall. I loved our visits, because my favorite cousin, exactly my age, was one of their four kids (three girls and a boy—Janice, Alice, Darleen and Erland). Janice was the oldest in her family, while I was the youngest in mine. Being dressed in either cotton pants or in dresses that our mothers sewed for us, standard fare for us young girls, did not stop us from climbing the trees or running around the yard and down the road and to the barn to see the animals. We took turns on the big rope swing, hanging a long ways from a high strong oak branch with a knotted loop to catch your foot in or to grab hard and high with your hands and run and pull your feet into the air. Back and forth in an arc we waggled, as long as our arms or feet could hold and the rope kept oscillating.

Aunt Celia, the youngest of the nine sisters, was short and stout, her girth always covered with a cotton print dress and sometimes a bib apron tied in the back in a bow. She was good-humored, unfailingly kind to all of us, and always ready with her hospitality. She kept a pot of soup on the back of her wood-burning stove. But we had no room for more food. We just whiffed in the steamy, sweet smell of vegetables and mild spices.

Sometimes, Aunt Ellen was there, visiting from her school in Madison. She was the most sophisticated of the Larson bunch, and I admired what she did to improve herself. She dressed and spoke well, was very engaging and enthusiastic, and had a sparkle in her eye—all desirable traits for a special education teacher, which she was. Ellen was single all her life, though she had a suitor for many of her early adult years. One of the top officers of the Green Bay and Western Railroad wanted to marry her. But he wasn't quite religious enough for her, and she said no. They stopped seeing each other, and for the rest of her life she regretted it.

On other trips we might see the three "spinster" sisters. Anna, Emma and Ruth were all spinsters, living in the Garden Valley homestead, Anna and Emma didn't have much money and didn't try hard to get it. But Ruth had a little more gumption.

I remember her as quiet and modest, a little heavy with a pretty face, but her tones were subdued, with no airs or dash or glitter to set the world afire. But she must have had some urge to explore the world. Unlike Anna and Emma, without gumption, Ruth had enough business sense to search out greener pastures for at least part of every year. Bravely, she ventured off to the big Twin Cities of Minneapolis and St. Paul. She found wealthy homes that, for her hard work and long hours as a housekeeper, gave her "keep" and a nice wage, which she stashed away for a rainy day. In the summers she returned to the farm homestead to help plant and harvest the crops. She would have married if she had the chance, but she didn't have a guy around who asked her. Whatever adventures she had had in the big city passed on with her when, at sixty-seven, she died of a heart attack. Bless her heart and my fond memories of her gentle spirit.

Anna and Emma, who lived together until Emma couldn't take it anymore, were odd. They both were what we might likely call obsessive-compulsive today. They didn't throw anything out. Old newspapers were stacked high on the floor and used to cover tables, dishes, and shelves. Anna cleaned the house ferociously. Emma tightened faucet handles so hard you could hardly turn them on. Anna became angry easily, and she sometimes yelled and screamed at family members, though not at my family. It was a little scary. As comic relief, Emma would say something that she thought was funny and then give us a coy laugh and smile and wink behind her black, round, horn-rimmed glasses. We thought she was fun. Emma had a boyfriend, Oscar, who took her around in his truck. They saw each other for many years until his truck and another car collided and Oscar died on the scene. People wondered why she never married Oscar, who was a perfectly nice guy. We heard that Emma was too scared to get married. She wanted no commitments, and she had Oscar's company when she wanted it. Maybe she was an early feminist. She did have love in her heart. She once wrote my mother, who was twenty-two at the time, in beautiful script in Sarah's small gold engraved autograph album, "Dear Sister Sarah—From morn till night may your life be bright. And misfortune never frown. May the sweet content of each day well spent. Be yours as the sun goes down—Your sister Emma." And even Anna wrote, "Dear Sister Sarah, When rocks and hills divide us and we no more each others see. Just take your pen and paper and write a line to me. Remember me as always your Sister Anna."

Anna and Emma came to Whitehall for frequent visits and trips to the doctor. They spoke Swedish with my mother, though my dad wanted to hear only English in our house. "We live in America, not Sweden," he said. They tried to keep the Swedish out of range of his ears. I didn't understand most of what they were saying, but the Swedish colloquial exclamation that I heard repeatedly and spoken with passion was "O! Segari! O! Segari!" "Oh my goodness! Oh my!" What a group of sisters my mother had!

That left Marie, born right after Emma and just before my mother. She did the most exotic of things. It impressed my young mind after the fact and opened me up to another existence. Marie met Rev. Victor Carlson at a church tent meeting, and they married and sailed off to China to become missionaries in the 1920s. The Home of Onesiphorus for Children, reorganized now as "Kids Alive" and no longer having a ministry in mainland

China, sponsored them. While it was the Home of Onesiphorus, Marie and Victor helped care for these children without parents, who were left on the orphanage doorstep. They taught them handicrafts, gardening, and caring for cattle, which provided them food, plus daily school for reading, writing, and arithmetic in Chinese. They raised the girls and boys (after communism took over and to this day, only girls are left at the orphanage doorstep because of the "one child per family" law and parents' desire to keep a boy to take care of them in their old age) to be Christian, and with that core of hundreds of children, they would hopefully convert the Buddhist and Taoist population in Ti'an to Christianity. (This was before the People's Republic of China was established and outlawed religion; the country became officially atheist in 1949.) Victor contracted tuberculosis and died in China. Marie buried him there and stayed on alone to complete the seven-year mission. She came back by boat to Seattle and was met by a man whom her father knew but she did not, and he proposed marriage right on the spot. She accepted his offer.

She carried with her to this country the beauty and mystery of China. When we visited the home of Marie Larson Carlson Matson and her three children in Alma Center (her husband Emil died in Birchwood), or as my dad called it, Punken Center, her artifacts were on display. Leone got to borrow some of the Chinese objects and a wooden shoe to show her fourth grade class in school. There was no statuary in Marie's home because of the Matson's literal interpretation of the Bible. The King James Version, Exodus 20:4, told them that "Thou shall not make unto thee any graven image, or any likeness of any thing that is in heaven above, or that is in the earth beneath, or that is in the water under the earth." Any effigies, figures, or statues were considered idols, and that was an abomination to God. But Marie's collection of elegant and colorful silk satin robes, embroidered slippers, chopsticks, and porcelain dishes and her Chinese Bibles transported me to a world and culture beyond my own, literally on the other side of the globe. Marie read daily from those Bibles, and she conversed in fluent Chinese with visiting Chinese friends the rest of her years.

Our trips home from visiting our aunts, all in Jackson County, were less than an hour, and the sun may have set along the way. The big red ball on the far horizon cast low, orange rays across the rolling green fields of corn and grasses—or covered in snow, if we ventured out in our car in the slippery, icy winter. The tin roofed chicken coops reflected the sunlight like a mirror, signaling the almost melancholy ending of a full day. Gazing at the beauty and mystery of the sunset, as if I were alone in that car, brought up all the big questions for me. I was the philosopher of the ages, wondering who and what and why was it all here.

Arvid and Sarah Erickson Wedding, November 1914

Ethel with 2 stars on cap for brothers in Service

DEBATE

E. Erickson, J. Hunter, J. Herness, A. Anderson, C. Mueller, D. Symicek, W. Amundson, Miss Harding.

1950 Freshman Spring

Ethel with H. S. Debate Team 1950

Ethel in smocked dress

Sister Leone and Ethel

Ethel and Mary Thorson, UW Madison Music Competition

Erickson Family 1947, row 1 – Leone, Sarah, Ethel, Arvid, Avis
row 2 – Raymond, Dallas, Sherman, Benjamin

Whitehall GB&WRR Depot

Train with coal chute on tracks

Ethel and Joyce in GB&WRR passenger car

Ethel, Leone, Avis, Dal, Sherm, Ray, Ben, Sarah, Arvid

Mother Sarah and Grandmother Sarah

Row 1 - Ethel and Cousin Janice
Row 2 - Aunt Lydia
and Mother Sarah

Ethel climbing wood pile

Arvid with 1st Baptist Church replica Christmas 1950

Ethel in curls on lawn   Arvid in Depot 1940

Arvid telegraphing in Depot

GB&W Steam Engine 1939   Arvid's car with mail-rack

GB&W Steam engine

GB&W Diesel locomotive

Kindergarten Class 1941, Ethel 1st row, 3rd from right

Baptist Daily Vacation Bible School 1941, Ethel 1st row, 1st on left

The Depot

STANDING PROUDLY ON A long stretch of turf, right square in the middle of my old hometown, is the Green Bay and Western ("Grab your Baggage and Walk," my dad said) Railway Depot. I have such affection for this edifice that thinking of it brings tears to my eyes. The memories fill my mother's diaries, my dad's writings, and my present immersion in the past. Mr. Arvid B Erickson, our dad, as the Whitehall Depot agent and telegrapher, carried its own pride for all of us.

This elegant, brown-brick, one-story building, with tall and wide arched windows all around to let in abundant light, was built in 1914, the year my parents were married. It replaced the original wooden-plank passenger and freight depot that was constructed, along with the steel tracks, in 1872–1873. The brick depot I know now and knew as a kid has a hip roof, with overhanging eaves and an extended open canopy beyond both the east and west outside walls. A three-sided bay window, facing a long cement platform close-up and parallel with the rails, allowed the agent to see trains coming and going east and west. The main office sat between two waiting rooms, one for women and one for men, with a bathroom for each. The freight room was on the west end of the depot. A cement platform supported and surrounded the whole structure. My dad said that it was very handsome and that everyone said it was the best-looking depot building on the whole Green Bay and Western Railroad Line

After seven years in Hustler, Arvid and Sarah and their two young sons took a brief break from railroading in 1921 to take up dairy and chicken farming, one of their "longings" during their courtship. But they found out they were not cut out for the farm, and by October of the same year, Dad was back in the railroading saddle, his first love, in Scandinavia, just east of the center point of Wisconsin. Less than four years later and two boys more, in 1925, they moved from Scandinavia back west to the Whitehall Agency, the best "trick" on the GB&W line between Green Bay and Winona, Minnesota. Arvid was beginning his new and final job that lasted for twenty-nine years, until his retirement in 1954. We three girls were born in Whitehall up to 1935, my year of entry, and my parents could then rest on their childbearing laurels. Arvid brought with him his own black Underwood typewriter and his telegraph key, both working items that the railroad did not provide, to set up in the depot. He put them on the spacious swath of built-in counters and desks that were already there.

His job was big. It was heavy with responsibility, endlessly demanding and important for government and business, especially in times of Depression and war. He helped deliver the goods—lumber, fresh produce, milk, eggs, chickens, larger animals, steel, oil, coal, and people, to name a few, seven days a week, twelve hours a day and more if needed. He kept the books, handled large amounts of money, carried heavy freight boxes, sent and received and delivered telegrams, and sold tickets to passengers—the list goes on. He was always well dressed in his high collared white shirt, plaid tie on the bias, dark tan pants, and a black-and-white-checked mackinaw jacket. We saw him at home morning, noon, and night for meals. In between, we could stop at the depot anytime and see him in action. And we did, almost every day.

At the exact six-month mark of my life, May 6, 1936—"eighty degrees" and a "real summer weather day," my mother wrote in her diary—Ben, Mother, and Leone took me in our Ford car to the depot. It was my first time there, to see my daddy and to get weighed. The freight scale in the freight room measured me in my clothes at seventeen pounds. Baby was dressed in the cap and sweater that Mrs. Jorgenson had given me, and I looked "pretty as a doll," according to my mom, which was special for my modest, soft-spoken mom to say. I was too young to recall those first impressions, but after many hundreds of visits, the memory of, as I called it, "Daddy's depot" is firm.

As soon as I got my sea legs at around age one, my mom and I walked downtown once or twice a day to shop and then to the depot. I watched my daddy sit at his desk by the bay window and type at his typewriter, click the telegraph key back and forth with his right thumb and index finger, listen for sounds being transmitted on the receiver that was swinging on a metal post above the level of the desktop, write or type down messages at what seemed rapid-fire speed, fill out "bills of lading," do paperwork, handle money, work with customers who dropped in to buy passenger tickets, bring boxes to ship, and pick up freight. He was honest, hardworking, and respected by all the townspeople and the railroad management.

When he first came to the Whitehall Depot in 1925 to start his job, ten years before I was born, officials of the railroad and auditors came on the number one train from Green Bay and met Arvid, who came in his car, at the same time. Together they walked into the depot. F. W. Bradison, the agent, came in after he was through with the train. He did not seem surprised that they were there and acted almost like he had expected them. The auditors took several days to straighten out the accounts and to check Arvid in. They were unable to locate all the items and collect for them. There was a shortage of around nine hundred dollars for the railroad and about one hundred dollars for the express company, and some money was short for the Western Union Telegraph. A representative from the bonding company also was there to see what he could salvage and to talk to Bradison about his difficulties. Dad thought that the job was too much for Bradison and that the management should have sent him not to that station, but to a smaller one. There was a lot to handle and manage. Such difficulties never happened to Arvid in all his years of railroading. His track record was clean as a whistle.

My mother dropped me off at the depot sometimes to see Daddy, and she would go to Dr. Tyvand or do some errand. I was well behaved and I just watched all the live action. How lucky I was to see my dad at work!

On my third birthday, a Sunday, Daddy took me to the depot alone. The rest of the family went to the Methodist Sunday school. There would be time enough in my life later for church. At home for lunch, we celebrated with friends and neighbors and gifts including a green glass baby plate from Daddy, cut with three partitions, that Mom bought at a sale the day before. I wish I had that plate now.

Baby chicks came by express to the depot in April 1938. It was my first time seeing the cute, fuzzy creatures, and I didn't know what to make of them. Mr. E. C. Getts would raise those chicks for his egg and poultry business. Some chickens became food for our table, but I don't think I made that connection. Other chicks grew up to produce eggs that we kids decorated at Easter time. We poked a pin in each end of the egg and blew the contents out into a bowl. Then we used a white crayon or a piece of white paraffin, used to cover Mom's jars of homemade jam and jelly, to make designs on the empty eggshell and dipped it in vegetable dye, which did not take to the waxed parts and revealed the designs we had made.

I was brought to the depot enough times that I knew the way, navigating it myself for the first time at age three. When we were old enough for school, my sisters and I stopped at the depot every day on our way home. The modern "visit your dad at work day" was every day for me. He always welcomed us and liked our being there, and he continued his work while we watched.

Other people dropped in on him, too. His tall, handsome, black-haired brother Harry, who was a missionary in Fredrikstad, Norway, and who during WWII, with the Nazi occupation of Norway, took refuge in Sweden, the land of his forbears, which was neutral during the war. He came maybe once a year to surprise Dad and have a good conversation in English. Dad refused to speak Swedish. The town ministers stopped in to be friendly and maybe invite and entice him to a special service, but to no avail. Dad loved to engage them in a debate about religious doctrines and dogmas. I learned how to debate by listening to him. Even at a young age, I was able to determine that my father won the argument every time.

Out of the Great Depression to which I was born grew many ideas about how to prevent another one like it. People saw the need to be assured of having money in retirement. Though Sarah was against unions before she even married Arvid, Dad did eventually rejoin the Order of Railroad Telegraphers. The railroad men, including my dad, were pioneers to work for a sound system of pensions for retired people on the railroads of the country. Leaders of the railroad union conceived and presented a solid plan to Congress that eventually passed and became the law of the land. Arvid was glad to have the chance to do his bit toward that effort. The railroad pension system was the impetus for Congress to push through the social security system that FDR signed into law the year I was born. Because of the union, Dad received a pension in his later years that Mother knew he deserved.

Steam engine locomotives were used on the GB&W railroad until diesel locomotives began to replace them in the early 1940s. I loved the picturesque "black iron horse" spewing smoke from its chimney and the sound of the whistle that warned us of the train's approach both day and night. The engineer actuated the steam whistle with a pull cord. Each engineer had his own style of blowing the whistle and could put his own form of expression into the sound. With the Doppler effect, when the train was coming, my ears heard the whistle at a higher frequency and pitch than when the train was going. At night, in my bed, I thought it had a mournful, melancholy sound, with a mist of the unknown. In the daytime, I felt fun and joy and comfort hearing the whistle tell me it was midmorning or midafternoon as I skipped down the sidewalk or sat at my school desk. Modern locomotives use a pushbutton switch, which eliminates the fine control over the way the whistle is sounded and takes away the mystery of what was to come.

There were also sad whistle sounds coming with a heavy cloud of the unknown ahead. World War II was raging in Europe and the Pacific when the United States entered the war in 1941. Those were weighty times at the depot and on the railroad tracks, with the comings and goings of enlisted and drafted troops as well as the transport of boxes for all uses from the Whitehall Box and Barrel Factory, foodstuffs including dried milk and refrigerated butter from the Land O'Lakes Plant in town, and meat made into Spam, preserved in a can and easy to ship to the troops. Meat, dairy products, and sugar were rationed in our homes and became "rations" for the men at war. Dad signed us up at school for the ration coupons and got a sticker for our front window, saying we were buying defense savings stamps and bonds. Avis worked, earning money and doing her civic duty, at the rationing board at the Village Hall. My mother got a five-pound canning coupon for sugar, and because she could hardly buy washing powder and laundry soap, she started making soap from lye and lard. Scrap iron was collected along the sidetracks because of the shortage of steel and iron and shipped to other states for making munitions of war. We all smashed empty tin cans to add to the heap. Because of the shortage of men, strong women were enlisted in the all-male railroad section crew, and they also filled the ranks of factory workers who made all those vital products shipped on the rails.

On Friday, July 31, 1942, thirty-nine boys left on the morning train for training. Dad said that it was not a happy crowd, but they tried to control themselves. "Sad indeed," Dad said.

The draft loomed for my brothers. My oldest brother, Benjamin, twenty-seven, was married with a child, and he worked as an agent-telegrapher in New London on the GB&W Line, an important job in the war effort. He was not drafted. Raymond, twenty-four, honored as the number one graduate of his chemical engineering class at the UW–Madison, was deferred by the local draft board in Whitehall because the Standard Oil Company of California had hired him as a chemical engineer to do important research work with aviation gasoline that contributed to the war effort.

My brother Dallas, eighteen, enlisted in the Marine Corps in March 1943 rather than waiting for the draft. On a freezing Sunday, March 14, just before Dallas left for the service, the boys went to the Methodist Sunday school, and we girls went to the Baptist Sunday school. Mother had a farewell pork roast noon dinner, and Dad, Mom, Avis, Leone, and I went to the school to watch Dallas and Sherman play a last basketball game against the Camp McCoy team. The boys won thirty-two to sixteen, a celebratory sendoff. After the win, back home, we had prayer, kneeling together in Mom's bedroom, and Dallas said good-bye. "It was so sad to see him leave," my mother said. A phrase from John 13 came to her: "and he went out and it was night." In the dark, Sherman drove Dallas and friends to Eau Claire, where Dallas left early Monday, March 15, on the 1:10 a.m. train from Eau Claire to Milwaukee, and then to a training camp in San Diego, and he eventually shipped to the Pacific. As the train pulled out, his last words to his brother Sherman and their crying girl friends, the Mattson twins, seeing Dallas off at the Eau Claire depot, were "I'll be back!"

Two days later, on March 16, 1943, a large crowd of people gathered at the Whitehall Depot to bid farewell to dozens of young men drafted from all over Trempealeau County and who were headed for war, my brother Sherman, twenty years old, among them. The draftees who gathered were my brothers' classmates and buddies, waiting to board the forenoon train to Merrillan and then on to Chicago and various training camps. Mothers, dads, sisters, brothers, and sweethearts all gathered around their own to spend their last moments with them. Sobbing women and anxious faces, fearful of the future, the men and boys putting on a brave front, filled the waiting rooms and the outside platform. My depot agent dad, whose fifty-fourth birthday was that very day, had to be brave too for his own boys and for everyone else filling the depot. These young men were facing possible death. "As made my heart both grieve and love," as my dad said, "to watch the sea of faces in the depot." I was seven at the time and in second grade. I saw all the drama around me and somehow imagined that they would all return. The train whistles had a mournful sound.

During the war in the mid-1940s, my dad had to deliver telegrams to the homes of parents informing them of their son's death. It was a tough job. As instructed by the war department, he always made sure that the husband was home so he could let him know first. Then the husband could let his wife know the news in the way he thought best.

He received and delivered, on September 2, 1944, the first war casualty telegram of many to come to the parents of Harold N. Stendahl, who had died while training. Archie Langworthy died at sea in the South Pacific on August 30, 1944, of a subdural hemorrhage while in performance of duty. Dad called Mr. R. R. Langworthy to ask him to come in to the depot. He had a telegram for him. He came in, cheerful as always and expecting an ordinary business telegram, and Dad said to him, "Mr. Langworthy, this is bad news for you." With a severe look at Dad, he slowly opened the envelope, reading it and rereading it, and he hit the counter with his fist and said, "Damn that man Roosevelt." When he regained his composure, he said, "Arvid, do you know my wife had a strange feeling, a sort of intuitive premonition about Archie the very day this telegram says he was killed?" Dad replied, "Yes, some women have an intuition in such matters, more so than men." Mr. Langworthy said, "Anyway, I am glad you called me first. Now it is up to me to tell her, and I don't know how it is going to turn out. I dread it." He walked out slowly. The world had collapsed around him, at least for the time. Archie was an only child. Several years later, Mr. Langworthy, whom Dad said had a genius for architecture, died of cancer. Mrs. Langworthy died soon after.

Ernest Moen was killed when the Belgian transport ship he was on, the SS *Leopoldville*, on its way to France with troops to support the Battle of the Bulge, was torpedoed by German submarines on Christmas Day 1944. Mr. and Mrs. Moen were both at home when Dad came with the ill-fated message. There was terror in Mrs. Moen's face as Mr. Moen opened the telegram and commenced to read it. Before he finished, she ran from room to room screaming, crying, and wringing her hands. Mr. Moen tried to calm her. Dad could do nothing about it. "He had performed his duty," he later said, "a sad one. The rest was up to them. It was their calamity, their misfortune, although no fault of theirs. It was sad indeed that they should bring up a handsome, tall and husky young man only to be killed in a senseless war that was brought on by the stupidity, greed and jealousy of a handful of selfish men."

Adelbert A. Bautch was killed in action on January 20, 1945. His parents lived on a farm a few miles out, and Dad had to hire a car and driver at the army's expense, as per their instructions, to deliver the telegram. A few days later, the Bautch daughter came into the office and told Dad that she was glad that her mother was not at home when the telegram came, which gave the family opportunity to arrange to advise her in a suitable way. When La Verne Hanke was killed, Dad again delivered the telegram by taxi to his folks on their farm. Omer B. Olson was killed in action on April 26, 1945. His parents lived in town, and Dad went to their door with the news.

Raymond V. Larson, a navy pilot at twenty-three, was lost in action and buried at sea on May 11, 1945. Dad delivered the telegram to his mother. His father had passed on years earlier, and Ray was her only son. She did not display any emotions, but it was a hard blow to her. Now she was alone in the world. "Personal tragedy!" my dad said. The Larsons and my family had been neighbors, and their Ray and our Ray were good friends from childhood and roommates as students at the University of Wisconsin–Madison, where, as my dad said, "they worked and dreamed together." He was married shortly before his death and left a grief-stricken wife as well as his mother behind.

Henry Engevold, twenty-nine, was killed in action on Okinawa on May 13, 1945. He was a tank driver in the Ninety-Sixth Infantry Division and died in the vicinity of Yonabaru Island. He was attempting to get a letter up to a wounded comrade during the company's attack on an enemy-entrenched hill when an enemy sniper shot him. Death was instantaneous. Henry was buried with full military honors in the Ninety-Sixth Infantry Division Temporary Cemetery Number 2, Grove Number 167, Row Number 6, Okinawa.

Because of the casualty telegrams, Dad was afraid he was coming to be somewhat dreaded as a messenger of bad news. He wasn't told as much, but he could feel it. Mr. Charles Keilholz, the county sheriff, stopped in the depot one day and told Dad, if ever he should receive a telegram for them, never to deliver it to his wife but to notify him and he would come for it when notified. "He wished to protect his wife," my dad said later, "as men have always tried to do in times past and at this time." Happily, Chuck's son came back after the war, sound and healthy.

Despair was never yet so deep,
In sinking as in seeming;
Despair is hope just dropped asleep
For better chance of dreaming.

All these names, and other armed forces service persons that died, along with names of survivors of the war, were listed on the Roll of Honor with their branch of service and a gold star at the end of their name if they were killed in action. That big wooden rectangle of six rows of names, with two panels of two rows each angled off to the sides and painted eagle wings spread out at the top and draped with the American flag, sat prominently on display for decades on the green expanse of lawn between City Hall and the bandstand and is now torn down, discarded and forgotten like the names on that display. Their names are resurrected with the annual reading of veterans who died in all our wars at a ceremony on Memorial Day in the Whitehall Cemetery.

Happily, there were no tragedies in our own family. On June 3, 1945, a neighbor came to tell Mother there was a long distance call for her. She went over, and it was Dallas. He had arrived in San Francisco that morning and would come home in about two weeks. She said, "It was so much nicer to talk to him when coming home, to what it was bidding him goodbye two years ago." On June 12, 1945, during his birthday month, he showed up in Dad's depot, earlier than he had told Mother, while Dad's nose was buried in books. Dallas said hello to my very agreeably surprised dad, He returned as he had promised the day he left home when he said, "I'll be back." Mother had just started making noon dinner, and she "heard a rap on the door and who could it be but son Dallas since he left us. I am so thankful that God brought him back safe." We were all glad to see him. Two months later, our neighbor Mrs. Stuve came over to tell Mom the good news that was on the radio at 6:00 p.m.: peace had been declared with the Japanese surrendering. My mother exclaimed, "I sure want to praise God for it, seems too wonderful to be true, hope that peace will last now." The milk plant whistled, and cars honked their horns. There were services in all the churches that night, and they were open all the next day for prayer.

Almost a year later, on March 18, 1946, Sherman sent a telegram when he arrived in San Francisco from India, saying it was great seeing the States and offering birthday greetings to Dad. Sherman returned home by air and rail. As soon as the train stopped in Wisconsin, he jumped off, knelt down, and kissed the earth. When he returned to Whitehall, my dad said they "were surely glad to see him and that both boys pulled through the war without a scratch." Mother said, "Sherman was a pretty happy boy, being free again, and we were thankful and happy to have him come home, Praise God for protecting care over Sherman and Dallas. God hears and answers prayers." After a glass of milk for Dallas and with Mother making supper for Sherman, the boys went on to watch the ball game at school. Dallas spent the summer working on the rails as part of the GB&W section crew, and Sherman had a stint helping his dad with reports at the depot and as agent and telegrapher there and at other stations. "My dear boys are back," Mother rejoiced.

To everyone's joy, many of their buddies survived, including Everett Everson stationed in Cairo, Egypt, and Conrad Johnstad, Dallas's buddy in the Marine Corps. Connie had served as a trumpeter in the Marine Corps Band and then as a rifleman and along with Dallas hit the beach on Peleliu Island in the Pacific. They had their time in foxholes and enemy fire and returned safe and sound from around the world and the perils of war. A benefit for their service was the GI Bill, giving my brothers free tuition and cost-of-living support for higher education, which they both pursued. By contrast, years earlier, the WWI veterans, by many people's figuring, had gotten "short shrift," with very small bonuses and a train ticket home. Decades after the war, at age sixty-nine, my brother Dallas died, and Connie played taps on his trumpet at his fallen buddy's memorial service in the First Unitarian Church in Madison, Wisconsin—a poignant and heart-breaking sound that brought tears to our eyes.

I was nine years old when the war was over in August 1945, and the men and women—the sailors, soldiers and marines and the WACS and WAVES— continued to return home to all the states in the Union. Jubilance was in the air, but the joy was tempered by the War Department numbers of around three hundred thousand American service people killed in action. A war was going on, so they were buried at sea or in military cemeteries in Japan, North Africa, France, Italy, Belgium, Luxembourg, Netherlands, and Great Britain. After the war, if a family requested it and it was feasible to do, the embalmed remains were dug up and shipped to the States in gray metal caskets placed inside a wooden box and then returned in railroad freight cars on the rails to their final resting place at home. The surviving servicemen and servicewomen filled the passenger cars. I felt joy because my brothers were home, and my parents were very happy and relieved.

The depot job was so heavy with work that Dad was on the verge of collapse with the strain of overwork—ten to twelve hours per day, Sundays included, due to the war and inexperienced assistance—and it continued long after the war stopped. He asked the railroad management for help and to be paid for his long hours (he was paid for only eight working hours). Essentially, they told him he could cut back an hour in the day, but he couldn't take his lunch hour, except on the run. So there was no gain. He took a year sabbatical, at a smaller wage, to become agent at the much less demanding station in Alma Center. He slept in his trailer next to the depot, was able to nap between trains, and drove home twenty miles twice a week for a day or two to be with his wife and family. We visited him often by riding the train to Alma Center. It was vital for his health to get some rest and reenergize, and then he returned to his Whitehall Agency. Two of my brothers took up railroading and telegraphy. Sherman helped Dad out and then started a second trick, 4:00 p.m. to midnight, at the Whitehall Depot and also worked at other stations along the line. Ben eventually became depot agent in Green Bay, the main station on the line, and also the management headquarters for the GB&W. Avis sometimes helped Sherman with the books while she was still in high school. We all took turns "collecting" on Saturdays for Dad from businesses that owed the railroad money for freight services. My sister Leone took me with her to teach me how to collect in June 1944, when I was 8 years old. We started a responsible job when we were young, and then the next kid down the line took over several years later. Being the last in the line, I collected during all my school years from age eight on. Avis and even Mother, who had more than enough to do at home, pitched in by washing the depot storm windows. For most of our time in Whitehall, working at the depot was a family affair.

In January 1943, with the war going on overseas, there was a near-tragedy on the home front. After the train had left the Whitehall Depot, Gunder Solsrud, forty-five years old, got buried in a heap of coal in the coal chute along the tracks. Rudy Hagan was right there to uncover his face so he could breathe and then to call the section crew. Dr. MacCornack rode the ambulance, and the fire department took an hour and a half to get him out and then to the hospital for an overnight stay. Mom had just gotten off the train from visiting some neighboring town and was in the depot, watching them a block down the line and praying. Gunder Solsrud survived. But picturing him buried in coal struck fear in my seven-year-old psyche, and the image has stayed strong in my memory all these years.

Other mishaps occurred along the line. Train 1 had seven cars run off the track by the town of Pray in April 1941. Train 20 derailed June 29, 1942, a half mile out of Manawa, near New London, one of Sherman's tricks. Twenty freight cars went off the track in the night. It took a couple of days to clear it up, and Sherman, as acting agent, was a very busy boy, as mom described it, with reports to get out. McGee, the president of the railroad, and other GB&W officials arrived and had their sleeping car, the 400, taken over to Manawa from Green Bay. All normal train traffic was stopped. A year later in August 1943, my mom and I left on the morning train, which was already two hours late, to go across the state to Green Bay to see Ben, who lived with his family in Casco. Just west of Blair, the train ran into a cow. It gave us a jerk, and we stopped. When we finally got going, we lost time all the way to Green Bay and arrived in the evening, missing our bus to Casco. We walked to find the Bacmart Hotel, where we stayed overnight for $1.50 for the two of us. We went right to bed after washing up and took the bus the next morning to Casco. Days later, going back home, everything was on time. I don't think that cow survived, but we did—and in good shape, with experiences building that propelled me to a lifetime of further adventures in travel.

Dad and Mother took me out of school in September 1942 to drive to Millston on the Omaha Road Line to see a train wreck and inspect the damage. They took me back to school in the afternoon. The next day Sherman, Mother, and I went again to see the wreck, and Sherman took pictures. Train wrecks and depot fires in other towns were a fascination that we often rode in our car to see. On April 19, 1946, the depot in the village of Taylor caught fire of unknown cause and burned down. The wind-driven flames jumped a spur track to set the lumberyard and the brine tanks in the nearby pickling plant afire. The volunteer firemen had to pull their nonmotorized equipment three blocks to the scene, and calls for help were made to neighboring towns. Smoldering embers were carried by the winds for a mile around, starting grass fires on surrounding farms. Garden hoses and bucket brigades saved the large pine trees and houses in the rest of the town. On his last trip into the burning depot, Edward Lambert, one of the volunteers, picked up a steel box of unknown contents—along with a dime. When they opened the box, they found over two thousand dollars worth of bonds and papers. I wonder if he saved the dime as a souvenir. Dad drove over in the evening after work to see the smoldering remains. The 20' x 40' depot was the third Taylor depot to be destroyed by fire since the founding of the town and the building of the first GB&W Taylor depot in 1873.

As a kindergartener in February 1941, I stopped at the depot at noon on my way to school with my valentines. I hid behind the unlocked door in the ladies waiting room to surprise Dad as he was coming in. He pushed against it quickly, and with the resistance of me behind the door, one windowpane broke out. Mom bought a new one for fourteen cents from T. B. Olson, and Dad put it in, with flakes of snow drifting down.

The Whitehall Depot was my haven all through my school years. Almost every day after school, I stopped in to see Dad. I stood on the other side of the ticket window, and Dad, in his walled office, asked me if I wanted a nickel for a 3 Musketeers candy bar from Fortun's Drug Store, and he handed me the coin as I nodded and said yes. I could put a penny in the gum machine on the wall in the men's waiting room and get a white and blue package of Chiclets, but I seldom did. I sat on the benches in one of the two waiting rooms and read books. I watched Dad talk on the telephone and file his train orders in a large, wooden, three-tiered file attached to the wall above his desk and another file attached to the end of his desk. From his brown wooden swivel chair, he looked out the bay windows and way down the rail line in both directions to see any approaching trains. He talked with customers and people just dropping in to have a conversation. Sitting across from him, I turned the tiny globe mounted on a short metal cone that sat on his desk, and I transported myself to all the places on earth. I gazed at the large, wooden, octagonal clock, mounted high up on the wall above his desk and next to the four-foot-high and three-foot-wide Northern Pacific calendar that showed all the months of the year at a glance and was printed on heavy white parchment. On cold-weather days, I sometimes came to the depot, only a block from school, instead of walking five blocks home to eat my lunch that my mother had packed in a brown paper sack. My dad was usually at home at noon hour, leaving his office door locked but the waiting rooms open, and I would eat my peanut spread sandwich alone, sitting on one of the long benches in the waiting rooms or hiding in one of the bathrooms if I saw any school kids walking by. I was afraid that they would see me through the large windows and wonder why I was there. I sometimes stood on the closed toilet seat and stretched my neck and head up to peek out the high transom window facing the shale road behind the depot, hoping no one would see me. When I thought it was near time for classes to start, I looked through the ticket window at the clock with Roman numerals high up on Dad's office wall, opened and closed the door facing the platform and rails, stepped down the cement steps, went around the depot to the left and then under the extended portico to the west, walked the gravel road past the two story, brown brick Whitehall Clinic that gave off an aseptic smell, even in winter, and returned to school.

One of the benefits of being depot agent was that our dad got free passes for all nine of us on the GB&W and on other railroads across the nation. After my first time riding on a train at age three with my mom to Arcadia, train travel became the most fun, natural thing in the world, like walking around the block. My brothers hopped on the train to go to basketball games and ski meets in neighboring towns. Other times they visited people they knew and then returned on the evening train. Occasionally, they took me along for the ride, and it was a thrill. Avis, Leone, and I would take the train eight miles to Blair or twenty-three miles to Alma Center to visit relatives or to walk around the town, eat our packed baloney sandwiches or buy food in the grocery store, and return the same day. Sometimes they would let me come back by myself while they stayed over with friends or cousins and got a car ride home later. By the time I was ten, my parents trusted me enough to ride the train alone or with a friend. I went to Independence or to Blair, walked around and looked in shops, bought a Bismarck in the bakery—all towns had bakeries—and rode back home. Dad knew he could telegraph the depot agents to find out my whereabouts, and he trusted that I was safe. What a sense of freedom and independence my parents allowed me to have so early in my life!

Those heavy steel trains, whose wheels were beveled with the smaller diameter toward the outside, rolled along on two sturdy steel rails. Day in and day out, the trains were pounding and lurching and breaking to a halt. A passenger car; coal cars; tank cars holding milk, gas, and oil; boxcars carrying animals, grain, and freight; a three-hundred-ton steam locomotive, and, last on the lineup but not least, a caboose (and sometimes two, if it was needed elsewhere) to bring up the rear—all weighing thousands of tons—weighed down the rails. The wheels rested against the jointed track that supported and guided the train. The rails were fastened to timber ties with steel spikes. The ties were buried in heavy crushed stone level with the earth. Terra firma was the ultimate bedrock support for the load.

From the time I could toddle, I stepped up from terra firma and onto one of the two parallel rails, and with Mother holding my hand, I managed a step or two. I watched Leone swing one foot over the other on one of the rails with ease. She could walk all the way from the depot past the tall coal chute to West Street without losing her balance and stepping off. Slowly over the months and years, I could almost run on that long ribbon of steel, following in her footsteps. Outside of town, my feet were on the rail as I looked down at the pink wild roses breaking through the pebbles between the railroad ties. I stayed balanced as I gazed out at the rolling golf fairways and putting greens to the north and farmer's fields of corn and grass to the east, west, and south, with the rails stretched out as far as I could see. What freedom I felt, and joyous abandon, holding my arms out like a plane's wings to keep my equilibrium and having the time of my life—walking on the rails.

The "best-looking depot building on the GB&W line," as my dad said, earned some well-deserved recognition. The Whitehall Depot was certified and placed on the State and National Register of Historic Places on April 19, 2006. From its birth in 1914 to my writing in 2011, it has survived in pristine condition for almost one hundred years, and it will—we hope and expect it will—with its honored, protected, and financially supported status, stand proudly for another hundred years and many more.

Early School Days

I THREW UP ON my first day of school. I was four years old when I entered kindergarten (one of a few public schools in Wisconsin in the '40s offering kindergarten) in the brown-brick, three-story rectangle sitting on a slight rise of ground and grass. Miss Gladys Nordquist, the classroom teacher, and Miss Peggy Donahue, the elementary music teacher, welcomed us to the left-corner front room on the second floor. It was September 3, 1940, a sunny Tuesday afternoon. There was no protest on my part to going. I had been in that building many times while still a toddler with my mother when she needed to speak with the principal or to teachers of my siblings, and I was impressed with her standing up for her children if there was any question about their behavior that she thought unfair. One day, before I started kindergarten, Mother and Leone met her third grade teacher on the street, and they greeted each other. Miss Hilgurt proceeded to tell them that Leone did not do a book report she was supposed to do. Mother said that she was with Leone when she read the book and did the report. "She's just afraid of you," Mom told her. Leone also has memories of a "dunce stool" in front of the class and the teacher pulling up students and holding them by the ear. Miss Hilgurt did not return the next year. She somehow lasted in the classroom until the year my mother told her face to face in front of my sister, "she's afraid of you." And there were probably a lot of other kids afraid of her too, afraid and unable to protest the harsh treatment. I wonder how much damage was done to tender psyches.

My kindergarten teacher, Miss Nordquist, was a nice lady and, unlike Miss Hilgurt, not someone to fear. My first friend in kindergarten was Rita

Olson. We were looking at books in the kindergarten library, and I vomited right there. I occasionally had the stomach flu, as Dr. Tyvand called it, and Mother recorded that faithfully in her diaries. But I think I felt the stress of too much newness—being part of a structured classroom for the first time and a large group of kids that had to stay together with no freedom to come and go—and I probably missed the comfort and security of my mom's presence. I took some pleasure that first day in building a post office with a clerk's window out of long, blond, shellacked wooden blocks and playing customer and clerk with play money, which I remember clearly, and on other days with stamps and letters that we brought from home. We sang "The Farmer and the Dell." But that wasn't quite enough to counter my stomach refluxing a protest. I might have stayed and soldiered on, but the teacher got my sister Leone, a fourth grader, to come and take me home.

After that inauspicious beginning, the rest of the year was a lot of fun. Even when I was not feeling well, I still wanted to go to school, and if my mom thought I should stay home, she sometimes served me breakfast in bed. One day our parents came to our classroom to see us present a program of nursery rhymes. Joyce Herness, my best friend from church and now my classmate, who had a lot of natural curls, presented the piece "The Girl with the Curl Right in the Middle of Her Forehead." We had a large shoe built for the program to represent "The Old Lady in the Shoe," and we were her children. The music, the art, and the make-believe in our play all were up my alley. I was quiet but socially aware enough to get along with everyone and smart enough to figure out what was expected of me and to accomplish any task. I enjoyed making music and pictures and using my words. School was over by 3:00 p.m., and sometimes I walked to the depot or home by myself. but Mom was home to find out about my afternoon. On my own, I learned to write cursive, and sweet Mother had me write a sentence and my name in her own diary. And she wrote at the top of another page "Ethel Mae is a nice, nice girl."

At the end of my kindergarten year in May 1941, Mom won a contest. Once in a while, our modest mother had a chance to show a hint of her smarts. She was shopping at Foss Store and stayed for the Quiz Game. "I was asked who was the Editor of the Whitehall Times, I said Scott B. Nichols, and of course was right, so got a $1.00 cookie maker and cake decorator in one, a very nice present." She then took in two auctions in town and did not buy a thing at either sale. That was her entertainment for the day.

Sherman graduated from high school, and we were all there except for Ben, who was on the other side of the state and sent him a key chain and a wristwatch, something Sherman had secretly wished for. Sherman, a fine speaker with a droll sense of humor, read the class will at the ceremony, and the next day, Memorial Day, Sherm, Dallas, Avis, Leone, and I all marched in the morning parade to the cemetery. The boys didn't know that they would soon be enlisting in the service and helping to fight a war. Sherm got a book, *Problem of Eternal Moment* by J. Grant Anderson, as a graduation gift from our aunt Marie, the missionary to China. And a card postmarked Salt Lake City, home of the Mormons, came from Uncle Harry, my dad's brother and a "two-by-two" evangelist, spreading the sect's religious beliefs in Norway in the 1940s. He had announced to all his siblings regarding his complete devotion to the "work" before going to Norway, "This is the real thing." That persuaded Harry's sister Martha and brother Albert to join up for their lifetimes. The rest of Harry's family, including his brother Arvid (my father-to-be), resisted Harry's missionary zeal and chose not to believe his religious message. Harry wrote in his 1941 postcard that he was visiting his and Dad's sister Anna Mae, who was moneyed by benefit of her husband, Ed Lichliter, in the pickle business. Harry was having a good time and traveling with his religious companion, Preacher Lawrence Dissmore, in the evangelism of the "two-by-twos." It was juxtaposition of time, war, religion, and philosophy, and, as in Sherm's book title, it was a moment in time, perhaps eternal because the moment is still going on with different flavors and players.

Ray graduated from the University of Wisconsin in the summer. I started picking strawberries with my siblings. And Mom started feeling less well. She exclaimed after drying out the play-tent in the yard and the bedding inside the tent, wet with the showers, "But how beautiful everything looks outside! Praise God for it all!" In the same breath, she said, "I felt weak today, got a dizzy spell after I came back from downtown after supper, could hardly walk from the front room chair to the couch on the porch, but soon got over it." The "not feeling so good" persisted though off and on for years. Dr. Tyvand didn't think there was anything seriously wrong with her, and she got some pills through him to thicken her blood (build up her hematocrit—the red cell/hemoglobin concentration). And she kept on peeling, canning, cleaning, and ironing.

World War II was raging in Europe in June '41. But the United States had not yet entered the war. So at home, we were living our normal lives, with Dallas enjoying driving a car-full of people with Dad after hiking at Castle Mound on their way home through Black River Falls. He drove into a telephone pole, broke the pole off near its base, and smashed the car's bumper, radiator, and more. Aunt Ellen rescued them in her Mercury, with Avis, Mom and me on our way home from Garden Valley, where we were visiting Grandma. Dallas felt so bad. But no one was hurt. All nine of us packed into Ellen's car, and she drove to Whitehall in a pouring rain. Dad and Mom replaced their old car as-is a week later with a 1938 green Ford Deluxe four-door sedan for $325 from Black

River Falls and drove it home again in the rain. On a Sunday afternoon in July, Dad took me, age five, out in the car to "teach me how to drive" (probably me steering while sitting on his lap) for the first time. Leone went along. The car survived, and so did we. I may have been too young for driving, but I wasn't too old for other wheels. Mom took Leone and me downtown and bought us a red, white, and blue Skyliner wagon. We used it a week later to haul three watermelons home from Galstads' Store. Ray left on the steel wheels of trains to get to a new job in California in August and a new wife-to-be in October. Both my parents felt sad about his leaving and wished he was not moving so far away.

Labor Day, the first of September, signaled the beginning of the school year. Dallas was at the top of the family heap now as a high school senior, Avis was a sophomore, Leone was in fifth grade, and I was in first. Miss Jeannette Kuettner was my first grade teacher. Our classroom was on the other side of the stairwell from the corner kindergarten room, both rooms facing Dewey Street. Good work habits—independence, promptness, initiative, and advantageous use of spare time, as well as not annoying others, being dependable, attentive, and courteous, and showing cooperation in work and play—were our school's written goals for first graders to strive for and achieve. Reading, social studies, numbers, music and rhythm, spelling, and writing were our school subjects. It all sounds good, but how would we measure "not annoying others" today, with different behaviors in different cultures and political correctness to modify the rules? Our growth in citizenship and in school subjects was observed by Miss Kuettner and reported on four times a year in written form and sometimes in conferences with parents. I was pretty much an S-for-satisfactory kid down the line, with a rare H for highly satisfactory (in reading) and a D for having difficulty (in talking and telling). I was a quiet kid, and thus the difficulty. And the better kid to not annoy others! Handwriting letters of the alphabet, words, sentences, and numbers for addition and subtraction and reading took up the majority of our time. The basics—reading, writing and arithmetic—reigned along with music. This was a musical town and still is, with performances bringing people in from around the county. Special class projects punctuated the week. A standout was the day we made butter. We put heavy cream in a glass jar and took turns shaking it until it turned into thick, white butter. It seemed a wonder that the liquid could turn into a solid with our input of energy, and if what we remember best from our past is a sign of its importance, making butter from cream was way up there with Jesus turning water into wine or Rev. Salseth, in one of his object lessons, turning clear water red by adding drops of a clear liquid (phenolphthalein) and adding a base (like sodium carbonate) to demonstrate the blood of Jesus that would save us from our sins. Then he magically turned the red liquid back to clear by blowing air into the glass through a straw (though the liquid could be toxic if ingested)—our sins were forgiven and disappeared.

On a Thursday in September, Mother made me a plaid dress trimmed with red to bring out the red lines in the plaid, similar to what Salseth did to make clear water turn red. We wore dresses to church, to parties, and to school, and even at recess when we played on the swings, the trapeze, and the merry-go-round. Mary Joan Klomstein invited me and other first grade girls to her birthday party, all of us in dresses, and I brought her a coloring book for nine cents. The next day, Friday, after sewing my plaid dress with red, Mom sewed a dress for Leone out of blue cloth left over from a dress she had made for our cousin Beulah. Leone took the GB&W to Blair to go to the annual September Egg Festival with her Blair friend Frances Dissmore. Later Leone needed to be picked up, so Dad left for Blair with Avis and me. I got in the car barefooted, so Dad bought me a pair of shoes in Blair for $1.39 and anklets for ten cents. We went again to ride the rides, including the Thunderbolt, at the Festival the next afternoon between Sunday church and the evening service. That was about as "worldly" as we got—to ride on a Thunderbolt and on a Sunday. That evening, dressed in my new shoes and socks and perhaps my new plaid dress, Ma and my sisters and I heard the Norwegian String Band at church with Rev. Otto Larson "bringing the message." The next night, at a special Monday night service, we four saw moving pictures of the Ozark Mountains, and a missionary talked about the work there. On another special evening a missionary couple from Africa showed moving pictures of people, animals, and buildings in Africa and pictures of the war in Europe. Mother said for all of us —Ma, Dal, Avis, Leone, and me—"it was good." Church was educational and entertaining, as well as delivering a "message."

Mother invited eight girls from my first grade class plus second grader Patty to a party for my sixth birthday on November 6. They gave me coloring books and crayons, a necklace, handkerchiefs, hair bows, a dime, and a Hi-Li mallet and ball with rubber cord attached from Rita Olson. I loved that mallet and ball and kept it a long time, along with my friends.

The day after my birthday my dad was biking back to the depot after lunch. The freight train was "switching," and when Pa tried to get across the tracks ahead of them, his bike got caught in the track. He tried to get it loose, but had to let it go as the train was so near. The bike got run over and "ruined a good thing," but "Dad escaped!" Mom said with joy. It was another birthday gift for the whole family. To replace his "wheels," Dad bought a cream with red, "like-new" bike from Harold Arneson for $16.

On December 8 we heard on the radio before dinner that the United States declared war with Japan. The next day President Roosevelt talked on the radio about the war, and Mom bought me a doll at Erickson's Store. I was an innocent six-year-old just enjoying the pleasures of childhood. A week later, we heard that men between nineteen and sixty-five had to register, and that men from twenty-one to forty-four would be drafted. With my brothers eligible, the war was hitting home just as we were starting to share Christmas greetings and to practice our parts for the Christmas programs at both the Baptist and the Methodist churches. Mother listened alone to the radio just before midnight New Year's Eve to hear them ring the old year out and the New Year in. The train went through at 11:45 p.m. and whistled an unusual lot of time, and she heard the noise of firecrackers going off outside at midnight. All the rest of us were asleep.

Throughout first grade, I walked usually three times a day to school and back with Rita Olson and Richard Hanson. On at least one eighteen-below-zero and windy January day, Mom let me sleep in, and I walked to school from our edge of town in the afternoon. Mother was sympathetic to really severe weather days and to our welfare. Leone, her friend Anita, and I walked to the clinic from school in early June of '42 for diphtheria and small pox vaccinations, a civic duty to not spread disease and sponsored by the school. Anita got sick. A week later Leone's vaccination leg looked terrible. Mom had Leone wait by the fire hydrant on the corner of our lot to catch Dr. Mac on his way to the clubhouse. He golfed there every night for exercise and conviviality. He told Mom to wet a towel with boric acid, put it on the leg, and change it every hour. I didn't seem to be bothered much with my shot. My parents would have skipped the shots, but the school more or less required it.

At the end of our school day and in the early evening, Leone and I watched Dallas and Sherman play basketball in the school gym. Dal was the high-score man when they won against Alma Center by nine points on February 25, 1942, with our Alma Center cousins Kenneth and Reuben Larson cheering on their own team in the stands.

Come May and warmer weather, Mother put up a white tent that she had cut and sewed (several years later she replaced it with a green one) with stakes to hold it in the ground under the spruce and pine trees in our yard for us to play in after school. Thanks to Dad and Dallas it was equipped with wiring for light and a radio. It became the clubhouse for our neighborhood friends to gather and talk and make plans. We girls started the "Jolly Girls Club." We set up weekly fees of two cents on Mondays and, at Clarice's suggestion, a free offering on Fridays that we would give to the Red Cross. We wrote a whole list of rules including "if a mess clean it up" and "if you have quit too much do not join again." Audrey and I set up a message system between our houses from her closed-in porch to mine with a double string loop and a can to put a message in. We reined it in like a fishing line. I saw my brothers playing chess and ping-pong with Alvin Windjue and other friends upstairs or in the basement of our house. But it wasn't all play, since we helped Mother with seasonal and daily chores. Any homework we had was not heavy, and we whipped through it, good students that we all were.

Every summer we went to Daily Vacation Bible School, sponsored by the Northwestern Bible and Missionary Training School in Minneapolis, for two weeks in mid-June. Avis, the oldest and very responsible sister working part-time jobs all over town, plus helping Mom a lot with work at home, was also one of the Bible school teachers when she was in high school and when she came home summers from Northwestern Bible College or Bob Jones University. She believed the tenets of the Bible as she had been taught and practiced it conscientiously. Mother was committed too. For at least one summer, Mom gave room and meals to two visiting teachers for two weeks. The Methodists and the Lutherans, as well as the Baptists, came to the Baptist Bible School, so I was with all my friends. Every day I played "Onward Christian Soldiers" on the piano in the front of the main worship room at nine in the morning, as everyone marched in from outside and filed into the pews. It was written in the key of E, which had four sharps, so I transposed it, playing it by ear, to the key of E flat with four flats, which was an easier key for me to play. I could really pound out a spirited take, with my long pinkie fingers and thumbs stretched a couple of notes beyond an octave as I got older, going up and down the keyboard with vigor. Without too much indoctrination, I think to accommodate the other faiths, we were taught Bible stories and drew pictures of Bible scenes, and we sang choruses, like "Climb, Climb Up Sunshine Mountain," with our hands and fingers "climbing" toward the ceiling, throughout the morning. We all had a good, fun time, and then we went home for lunch and the joys of the rest of the day.

The summer was a time to play. I loved and was good at setting up and playing croquet, with the wooden mallets and balls and wire hoops to push into the ground, in our front yard. We played jacks sitting cross-legged on the sidewalk. Audrey Stuve and I had marathon sessions, playing Monopoly with Clarice Bautch in her glassed-in front porch all day with breaks for eating lunch and checking in with our moms. I played Sorry with Patty Hegge in her extended attic with four dormers and a finished wooden floor and in her large sunroom, the shape of a circle, which extended out from the corner music room and porch of her big two-story, red-brick house. We also cut out paper dolls that looked like Sonja Heine, the Swedish skating Olympian, June Allyson, and Ava Gardner, the movie star I saw years later in my first forbidden-by-the-church Hollywood movie, *Show Boat,* in New York City's Radio City Music Hall.

To cool off in the summer heat we kids dunked in the round, cement pool behind Patty's house. At night the neighborhood boys and girls gathered under the light of the lamppost on West Street in front of the Hegge's lawn and played kick the can, hide-and-seek, sardines, and run sheep run. After an hour or two, our moms would call us to come home, except for Clarice and Jackie's mom. Jackie, the same age as Leone, said to her years later that she always envied her that our mom cared enough about us to call us home.

My sisters went to Bible camp the end of July, and on the same day Dad's sister, Martha, who had introduced Dad and Mom to each other in 1914, came with her husband and kids and niece from Janesville to visit through the next day. I liked them. They were all pretty and handsome and nice and smart in the ways of the world. I always observed or learned something useful from them about piano playing (my cousin Evelyn became a concert pianist), the fashionable clothes they had on that I might be able to sew someday, their unusual "two-by-two" religion that met in homes, and their ideas on how to run a very successful nursery business, Fairview Nursery, which they owned.

Men from around the county started leaving on the trains for war training camps that summer of '42. John Johnson and Ray Larson enlisted in the Air Corps in July and August, respectively, a year after we entered the war in 1941.

Mom and I rode the trains, also, to Alma Center and relatives and back and to other towns. Dad and Mom and I went in our Ford car to Camp Chetek to pick up my sisters, and Dad took us to county fairs in Black River Falls and Mondovi, where we indulged in pink cotton candy and watched the demolition derby of cars, both of which did not make me feel good.

I climbed the spruce trees lined up on the west side of our yard, the first one in the line facing Blair Street being my favorite, and I sat like a Buddha on a high, strong branch and contemplated the world. I took long walks with my dad in the country pastures along the fence lines, all the way to small Lake Alagoochie, a depression in Henrik Herness' rolling pastureland, while Dad made me a whistle. He would find a thick stick along our path and whittle it with the pocketknife he always kept in his pants pocket. And the glorious summer came to an end.

On a cloudy Tuesday, September 8, 1942, we three girls started another school year. Ben and Ray were long gone, and Sherman and Dallas were out of school with jobs. Sherm was a traveling relief agent on the railroad, and Dal worked in the shipyards of Seattle, Washington, until they entered the service the next year. Avis was a high school junior, Leone was in sixth grade, and I, the last of litter, but becoming seasoned to this classroom thing, entered the room next to the one from last year's.

Miss Elouise Torkelson was my second grade teacher. Lucky for me, she, too, was very nice. We learned to multiply and divide numbers and to write cursive. I got a lot more H's than in first grade, in ten listings under growth in citizenship and in fifteen under growth in subjects. Except for a rare Mrs. A. B. Erickson signature, Dad signed all the reports, all four periods in all my years of school, with "A. B. Erickson," the *n* flowing in a swirl and swoop to the bottom of the page. As part of our civic duty, Leone and four other girls collected scrap iron and rubber for the government. Mother gave them four springs, a folding bed, skates, and rubber tires that they took in several trips to the side rail by the depot, in another use of our patriotic red, white and blue Skyliner wagon.

Patriotism and civic duty also manifested as voters showing up at the polls. We had some awareness of politics because of Dad telling us what was happening in the news. He voted for whoever was "the best man" in his estimation, as president or senator or whatever, but it was more often than not a Democrat. Mother more often than not voted the opposite party from Dad. They did vote conscientiously, but their votes usually canceled each other out. They did not argue about their different political or religious views. Both of them frequently stated their beliefs, but there was never a contentious debate or upset. Mom put a high value on keeping the peace. As she wrote in her letter to Arvid during their courtship, "Hope that you and I will always live peacefully together." And they did. They seemed to quietly respect each other's views and see the good in how they both lived their lives and raised their children. For we kids, that was splendid. We saw a range of beliefs, sometimes evolving, held without any wrangling or bickering. No one had to be right. It was all the better for us to evolve our own takes on the big questions.

After noon dinner, on November 21, 1942, Mom and Dad's twenty-eighth wedding anniversary, Dad drove Avis, Leone, and me to Winona to take in the speeches of three governors for a dedication of the new bridge that crossed the Mississippi River. But because we found out that they had made their appearances in the morning, we went shopping instead, and Avis bought a very patriotic red, white, and blue plaid skirt and a blue sweater. And Mom, at home, went to an auction that must have been over and done with because no one was around, and she continued on to see a friend who was not home. So she went back home, took care of the fire and laid down to rest.

In the new year of 1943 there were carnivals at school and parent-teacher nights, and Mom and Leone would listen to me play triangles as well as castanets in the rhythm band. We would also watch moving pictures of news events and be served lunch for ten cents each.

I watched Mom dye rags maroon for her hooked rugs, and as soon as the ground was thawed in April, we all pitched in to dig up her flower and vegetable gardens, hoe, plant seeds, and put in seedlings, and in the evening, we spaded to loosen the soil and get up the weeds. By late summer, we were pulling up vegetables, shaking off the dirt, and eating them raw right in the garden.

Ben came home for visits with his family from Winona and then from Green Bay and showed us movies and slides that he had taken of them and sometimes us. It was pretty special to have movies in our house, especially since movies at the Pix Theater were off-limits. At age seven I went with some friends to go downtown on a Saturday evening and came home to find out that he had shown movies without my knowing he would and that he wouldn't show them again. I said to Ben, "I wanted to see it. I was coming right back." I felt so bad, and I went into the kitchen to bear my sadness away from the others. Leone, around eleven, followed me into the kitchen, put her hand on me with sympathy, and said, "I understand how you feel." She had thought that wasn't nice that I couldn't see the movies and had said, "Ethel's not here. Don't you want to wait for Ethel?" But they went ahead anyway. She felt real bad for me even before I got home. Her empathy when I felt so down stayed strong in my memory.

The summer flew into the fall of 1943. With my brothers Sherman and Dallas both in the service, we hung a two-star flag in our porch window facing the street, and it was time for me to join the combined third and fourth grade class across the wide hall from second grade and facing Hobson Street, taught by the dark-haired, tall, "ever-lovin'," as we called her later, Miss Janet L. Lentz. She didn't feel so lovin' when she poked your head with her long, red-polished fingernail and a piece of chalk for no reason. Nancy Boll got away with anything and everything, we all thought, from kindergarten on. She was our school Principal Gus C. Boll's daughter, and she could lord it over us. She chewed her fingernails, so the teachers let her chew gum, forbidden to the rest of us. The good thing was that I was glad I didn't chew my fingernails and that, unlike my sisters, our class did not have Miss Hilgurt and her dunce stool. Nancy Boll did come to my birthday party the next year and gave me paper dolls. Mom gave seven of us girls, Shirley Mae Lee, Rita Olson, Joyce Herness, Georgia Staff, Suzanne Benson, Nancy, and me, a full supper of mashed potatoes and gravy, roast beef sandwiches, chocolate cake and the birthday cake besides, and milk and orange juice to help wash it all down.

To tend to health needs, Mother took Leone and me after school to Dr. Tyvand's office for free exams through the school. Dr. Tyvand said that one of Leone's tonsils was affected some, and he suggested that I have both of mine removed and that Avis, a high school senior who was examined earlier, should have something attended to. Mother was against surgery, so Leone and I escaped the knife and were fine. Avis, however, a dozen days later, walked to the hospital alone early on a freezing December morning to have a growth in her breast cut out. Dr. Mac called our neighbor (we didn't get a telephone until I was in high school) for Mom at home to come and have a look at the growth before Dr. MacCornack sent it to the lab in Madison. Avis was fine, but Leone felt for her that she had to go it alone. We were all supported and nurtured in many ways in our family, but we were often on our own in tough times. Our parents had had it way tougher in their youth. It was another case of not coddling. But Dad, Mom, Leone, and I visited Avis when she was awake and talked with her, so she felt family support. And Dad did bring her home two days later.

After coming home from the community Christmas party in 1943 I asked, "Ma, don't you wish you had gone there to see Santa Claus?" and I showed her my big bag of candy. Ma said "No. The rest that I had while you was gone was worth more than that." Then I said, "Oh, no. You have to wait another year before you can go and see Santa Claus, but you can rest a million times before then." At the end of the year it was a tradition for us girls to celebrate New Year's Eve and bring in the New Year at a party in the Baptist parsonage. Mother said, "Thanks be to the good Lord for the past year. May I have been at least a blessing to someone."

Our parents and teachers did not make it easy for us. In third grade and eight years old, I walked to school alone in the early-morning darkness, on a barely above-zero morning in January to give Miss Lentz a written report on a book.

Miss Lentz said our class was slow to learn time (though wasn't going slow a kind of time?). So she brought in Donny Myen from first grade, whose dad was Dr. Myen, a family doctor in the clinic who had moved to Whitehall a year earlier in August 1942. Donny had learned time fast and at an early age, and he showed off his skills. Well, being humiliated might be a motive to learn, and I know kids in that class who did have a hard time with time. But we all learn about time eventually—and maybe all too soon in this life, we learned about the pressures of time: meeting deadlines, pondering the future, and sometimes regretting the past. Numbers from our early years became arithmetic in third grade. And in spite of our lack of ability to read the clock, we did learn to multiply and divide bigger numbers. Years later I called Miss Lentz a favorite teacher.

After eating my bag lunch alone at the depot for many weeks, I decided to start going home for noon dinner. My mom was always entertaining and preparing food for us and others—for the prayer meeting group or the Dorcas Society coming to our house or friends and aunts and cousins from other parts who frequently dropped in for dinner and supper. I could have eaten hot lunch at school for sixty cents a week or have had my bag lunch with my classmates lined up on a bench in front of a counter. I had brought my lunch several times, but I was embarrassed to have them see my homemade bread instead of the Sunbeam bread from the Farmers Store that everyone else had. It took me years to realize how lucky I was to have bread that my mother made.

After school, Avis, Leone, and I went to basketball games in the school gym, even without our brothers in school to be on the team. Mom and I went to the Village Hall to hear Leone play French horn in the school band and to see her march in her orange and black uniform, playing her horn, in the Memorial Day parade through town. We all had turns baking cakes and cookies and making chocolate fudge after school to mail to our brothers or to bring to church gatherings, engagement showers, and school events. I mailed Avis's valentine cake to Sherman in the service in Austin, Texas. Sherman wrote, "believe you me it was good and the men in the office ate it with home brewed coffee." He guessed that Avis had made it. I had the initiative and freedom at age eight to come home from school one day, look up Sonja Heine cookies in Mother's *Good Housekeeping Cookbook,* and to make and bake and mail them to Avis in Tennessee. I had just gotten two new sets of paper dolls, "Victory" (six dolls representing all branches of the armed services with a wardrobe of clothes), because I had brothers in the service, and "Sonja Heine" paper dolls—and I was inspired to bake Avis cookies. They were pretty, with chopped walnuts coating the outside of the ball and a dollop of jelly in the depressed center, and they tasted good with the sweetness of brown sugar. I mailed them to Avis with a letter saying, "I'm sending you yummies I made all by myself."

I played almost every day with my closest neighbors, Audrey Stuve, Clarice Bautch, and Patty Hegge. Roger Olson, the Grover boys, and Rita also came over for fun and games, like drop the clothespin in the bottle, Flinch, Old Maid, and Rich Uncle. We lived in the glory days of little homework pressure, with free time until supper or bedtime. On May Basket Day, May 1, we girls were busy receiving and giving away May baskets. We folded them out of wallpaper sample book pages and pink napkins, added paper-fold pockets to put in candy corn and gumdrops, and attached paper handles to hang off of people's doorknobs. They were in a beautiful array of colors and designs and shapes. Avis graduated from high school on May 18, 1944. The diplomas didn't come, so Mr. Boll handed out rolls of blank paper instead.

I went to Bible camp for the first time that summer, at age eight. In July, from Monday to Monday, the Baptist kids went to Chetek Bible Camp at the Lutheran campgrounds for one week. Rev. Salseth, Dad, and other parents took Avis, Leone, Joyce Herness, Gwen Thompson, the Grover boys, the Lockman girls, and me and our trunks filled with bedclothes, our clothes, and our Bibles in their cars. Rev. Salseth had a rack on top of his car to hold the luggage that didn't fit in other cars. Living in unfinished cabins, sleeping on bunk beds lined up in two long rows, and walking down the pine needle and tree-root-filled path to the girls' bathroom with no-flush toilets in the dark made for rougher living than we were used to, and it was fun from the get-go. Tall, dense pine trees filled the rolling grounds. Beautiful Lake Chetek was at our doorstep, and afternoons were for boating and swimming, though I didn't know how to swim. I dunked, floated, and tried to swim, afraid of putting my head in the water. At home every summer my friends and I cooled off in the Trempealeau River at the foot of the dam by Hegge's Feed and Mill Store. If I lost my footing and went under, I came up gasping with fear. At least Lake Chetek was not churning with a falls overhead, but I still didn't learn how to swim.

The morning camp class offerings, such as "False Creeds and Cults," were held in cabins or sitting on the needle-covered grass under the towering pine and spruce trees, and the evening services were in the open-air auditorium. Both the courses and the services were heavily evangelistic. The leaders were hell-bent on getting us saved. I was an early skeptic. "How is it decided and who decides what creeds are false? Maybe this Baptist creed is false by the same standards. What makes a cult a cult? Why isn't the body of beliefs we are being told is the truth also a cult?" I wondered, but hardly dared to ask. My Dad's skeptical, questioning, debating (but not indoctrinating) ways were in my head. I did dare to ask one minister in church later if there was a universe beyond the one he and the Bible said God created. I was given a look of disapproval, asked how I could even think such a thing, and offered no adequate answer. Leone told Mom the year before I went to camp that about fifty kids got saved at Junior Camp Chetek. One boy did not take much interest in classes until after he got saved. Then he changed and was so happy. "Praise God, therefore," my mother said. Many kids went forward at the end of the evening services that I attended when the plea was made to come and ask Jesus to forgive your sins and to take him into your heart and be saved. We sang "Just as I Am without One Plea" time after time with a pleading, heart-rending sound. "But that Thy blood was shed for me, And that Thou bidd'st me come to Thee, O Lamb of God, I come! I come!" Through five verses and again we sang, with kids making a decision and leaving their bench to go forward, the piano playing and pleading too, it seemed. My head was in turmoil with my questioning thoughts and the dense emotional weight that gripped the hall. These were good people who lived a good life with morals to guide them, and I couldn't reject that. I straddled the line, but did not go forward. The week came to an end and we were picked up and dropped back to our former lives, a little more savvy in the ways of religion. I was a little worn with the uncertainties of so many beliefs but felt good with all the fun we had.

Miss Lentz was still at the helm when I entered fourth grade in the fall of 1944. School always started the Tuesday after Labor Day, this time on September 5, a cloudy, seventy-degree day. We launched into the same subjects: arithmetic, reading, writing, spelling, music and rhythm, and social studies.

Infantile Paralysis or polio was a scare that year. It started in the summer, with news in the *Milwaukee Journal* that I bought at Fortun's Drug Store on Sundays at Mom's request. Young people across the country were becoming paralyzed with a strange virus or infection or something that started out like the flu. The Whitehall coach, Mr. Colonel Larson, got it, but he recovered over time. When the thirteen-year-old Maule boy was not feeling good at school and his leg became paralyzed in September, it got our attention. He was taken to the La Crosse Hospital. The schools and the Pix movie theater closed, and then churches closed for a couple of weeks in a row, which was pretty remarkable in itself. We normally went to church come hell or high water. About the time he got sick, mid-September, I did not feel well, and I had a couple of dizzy spells as I described it in a letter to Avis. I stayed home from school. A week later, I had a stomachache and headache in the morning, threw up and didn't eat, and got feverish in the late afternoon, so Mother called Dr. Tyvand, who came and said I had the stomach flu. "We were so afraid that she would come down with the Infantile Paralysis, but was soo glad it wasn't," my mom wrote. And the next day, "Ethel Mae is feeling much better today, which I am so glad of."

That same day in September '44, Dallas wrote from the war in the South Pacific,

> Imagine Leone and Ethel are on the start of another school year. I envy them. I plan on taking advantage of this government education program sometime after the war is over. I won't be writing again for quite awhile so don't worry if you don't hear from me. That isn't your cue to quit writing me though, cause I'll be looking forward to hearing from you. Love to you all. Dallas, Pfc M.D.Erickson.

He was helping fight a war, but his heart was at home, and he was looking toward the future. But soon after, we did receive another letter from him, describing the landing from his ship on the high seas on the island of Peleliu. His outfit went ashore in the rain, slogged through the mud for two hours with all their paraphernalia, and set up a temporary camp, with fighting going on a short ways away. Dal had a good chance to make use of his Boy Scout training in setting up their shelters and making fires to heat the rations. He said it was a lot of fun, in a way, but not very convenient. He looked around for his buddy, Connie Johnstad, who had been on another ship and found him on a truck. They were pretty glad to find each other out there, and they shot the breeze back and forth for quite a spell. A bunch of them got sniped at, and they got in a foxhole that night. "I am feeling swell," he wrote, "and don't worry about me. More later. Love Dal, P.F.C. M. D. Erickson 10-2-44." Later, artist that he was, he sent drawings he made of some of his buddies. Sherman, meanwhile, sent five letters airmail from India, five days in a row, and one was for me on my ninth birthday—to me alone, as I requested of Avis and my brothers in my letters to them. Sherm said he worked the night shift in the Union Telegraph Office in Assan Province and that his unit hired a native boy they called Curly to keep their uniforms clean and pressed and to help prepare their "very good chow, but no fresh milk or eggs or steaks of course."

In October of that year, Marie Rice, Leone's classmate, got polio. Her mother was the Latin teacher in high school, and I took Latin from her when I finished elementary school. Marie had played the piano and violin beautifully, and now her arm and her legs were paralyzed. Over time, she recovered enough to use crutches and to slowly get her body from place to place—and even better, to be able to play her precious instruments again.

Dad managed to get a week's vacation that October and, after driving around Wisconsin a couple of days, he wrote Avis in Minneapolis, saying, "All I am doing since I came home is sleep, eat and loaf. So far I have gone to bed 20,075 times. And I have eaten 60,225 meals, more or less. And I have been here 481,800 hours, more or less, if you like statistics. Well time to go to bed. 73-Regards, Love-Dad. 'The Old Man.'" Dad was fifty-five and well deserving of a break from the heavy work and long hours he put in at the depot.

I wrote to Avis to thank her for her card to me on my ninth birthday and said, "We have a new boy in our school. One arm is shorter than the other. His hand comes out at his elbow." And, "Write to me alone please soon. Mother said that she wasn't going to send you anything more until you say thank you. Love, Ethel." That boy was our fourth grade classmate Charles Jacobson who years later became prom king.

Grandma Sarah Larson, eighty-two years old at the time, stayed with us in the fall of 1944. She wasn't feeling well, and I told Avis in a letter that I had to cheer her up. Grandma knit me a pair of red mittens and told us on Dad and Mom's thirtieth wedding anniversary, November 21, 1944, the day she finished the last thumb of the mittens and returned to Garden Valley, "I believe this will be my last knitting." It was. Eleven days later, on December 2, Dr. Tyvand drove Mom and me in the middle of the night to her farm, and she had died of a heart attack thirty minutes before we got there. She lay on her bed in the old homestead bedroom off the kitchen, perfectly still, and I felt forlorn. It was an early experience for me with the reality of life —death. I had just turned nine. The day before Grandma died, Mom recorded that I took my very first piano music lesson, at fifty cents a lesson, from Mrs. John Jacobson after school. I'm sure my music was a comfort to me as I had tried to be a comfort to my grandma in her last days. I kept the red mittens, and decades later I gave them to my own daughter to wear. My mother said, "May we meet her up yonder is my earnest prayer."

When the school showed a movie to the whole grade school in the wide hall between the classrooms, it was usually the news of the week or month with Edward R. Murrow, an American broadcast journalist, reporting from the war zones and sharing political, medical, and weather disaster news. I did wonder then how my two brothers were faring and somehow trusted that they were out of danger. Once in a while, our class walked to the movie theater near the tracks to see a more "worldly" movie from the likes of Hollywood, and I, with a strong conscience, even though I questioned most of the church's tenets and doctrines, had to decide if it was "too worldly" for me to see as a Baptist. One day at the end of January 1945, when I was still in fourth grade, I decided I shouldn't go to the show that the class was going to, and I walked home—or as my mother said, "Ethel Mae preferred to come home." In my own diary I said that I came home at 1:30 because the school was going to a show. Joan Roseland, the Dokkestuls, Carol Rene, and Joyce, all belonging to the Baptist Church, didn't go either, and they came home with me. Joyce's dad, Henrik Herness, went to movies in Independence and Blair but avoided them in Whitehall so as not to be found out by the Baptists. Our dad went at least once to the Pix, but he didn't want Mom to know. Leone, in high school, couldn't go home but sat alone in the study hall after the rest of the class went to the movie. She won first prize for selling the most tickets to a school event, and her prize was a ticket to the Pix Theater. She said no to the teacher when offered her prize.

With our loyal practice of and immersion in the Baptist teachings of the Bible, reading it from cover to cover and memorizing and reciting of many Bible verses, I wrote Avis in February and told her that the longest verse in the Bible was Esther 8:9, the shortest was John 11:35; the shortest chapter was Psalms 117, and longest chapter Psalms 119. Being an excellent student of the Bible, Avis probably knew that already, but I wanted to share the excitement of my knowing. We girls, maybe even more than our brothers, were well schooled in our religion.

In March 1945, our public school classroom flooded, and we went home. Was it freezing pipes in the eight-above weather? After noon dinner, we went back for class in the music room, which would have suited me as our permanent classroom with all the inviting musical instruments on wide shelves jutting out from the south wall of the room. Starting March 21, I stayed home a week with a cold, and early on I asked Mom to order two medical books for me through the mail to spend my time reading. They had given me a doctor's set for Christmas when I was seven. Now at age nine, I continued to be fascinated with the health of the body and the workings of disease. It became a life-long pursuit, though I never went to medical school. Girls were not encouraged to reach that far. After a week, I walked to the clinic to get a permit from the doctor to go back to school. The school year was not winding down but revving up with red-letter day events to come.

To a shocked nation, President Franklin D. Roosevelt died on April 12, 1945, at age sixty-three. On Tuesday, May 8, 1945, the Germans surrendered and VE Day, Victory in Europe, was declared by President Truman. In celebration, Mom, we kids, Mrs. Henrik Herness, and Joyce and Audrey Stuve met at our house in the afternoon, with school off to celebrate the end of at least part of WWII, to measure out cloth for our costumes for the grade school's big operetta. Joyce and I, as well several others, were to be bluebells, with other girls appearing as a bunch of roses with pink dresses and a bunch of daisies with yellow dresses with white trim. The boys were to have green suits for foliage. The next day, five of us neighborhood girls walked to school together carrying our bluebell, rose and daisy dresses with us on hangers. "Sure looked pretty as they walked along," Mom said. She had what might have been a repressed talent with her housekeeper role, except for her artist's eye and skill that came through in her sewing and in her flower gardens, tagging them with fabric scraps to match the color of the flowers as a reminder of her color arrangement. Mother also had an eye for finding four-leaf clovers that she pressed in her diaries on the date that she found them. A day later, the grade school performed the annual grade school operetta, directed by Miss Peggy Donahue, the elementary music teacher, for the high school with our "garden and rainbow" clothes on. The next night we played Village Hall, and both my mother and my father were there. Leone sang with a group of others. I felt shy and sweet and pretty as a bluebell dancing across the stage with the other flowers and happy that my parents were there.

For a last class project I made a birdhouse with Dad's help in the basement workshop, and I painted it red to take to school. "The old man comes in handy twice in a while, eh?" he would say. I brought Mother's scalloped corn to our fourth grade picnic in the John O. Melby Park, and fourth grade was over on Friday, May 25. The farmers needed their kids home from then on to help with crops and chores throughout the long summer. June 4 was that memorable, landmark day that most kids have and that I inscribed in my diary: I learned to ride a bike. I went to meet my cousin on the bus for her to start Bible school with me, but Janice was not on it, so I met the evening train instead with Janice's bike on it for my use. I practiced to ride the rest of the evening. What a glorious feeling it is to catch the balance and take off and realize the world is yours for the taking! I kept practicing through the week, and that Saturday I took Janice's bike to the depot to be sent back to Hixton. I fell several times at first and got two skinned knees and bruises on my hip, but I said in my diary that "I could ride pretty good now." The injuries were a small price to pay for a lifetime of a newfound freedom. Patty and Leone took me places throughout the summer on Patty's bike and on our boys' bike, passed on from our brothers, who had bought it with their newspaper delivery money.

We were happy and relieved when Dallas came safely home in June from the South Pacific. But Mom was concerned about his being wayward from the ways of the Lord. I even wrote in my diary, "Dal fools around so much at night sometimes until 3 o'clock." I also said, "meany Dallas dropped Mom off from the car at the grocery store and didn't wait to bring her home carrying all her groceries." Mother spoke with him one evening about living for the Lord and not to be out with worldly people but to take an interest in Christian people instead. He said that he had been preached to so much that he was the most conscientious one in the bunch, and Mother was glad that he felt that way about it. She said there are just two places, hell and heaven, told him to live right, and said that she did not wish any of her children would go to hell. "Don't worry about that, Mom," he said—which meant that her children wouldn't be going to hell.

The war was not over. Dad took Leone and me to Blair in July to go through the pea factory. Three German war prisoners were working there. It gave me a strange feeling to see them working hard and quietly and not meeting anyone's eye, away from anything they knew and kept prisoners with no freedom to come and go. On Monday, August 6, 1945, an atomic bomb destroyed Hiroshima, Japan, killing 343,000 people, as it was reported on the radio. The next day I recorded in my diary that a test of an atomic bomb had been conducted in New Mexico on July 16. At noon on Thursday, August 9, we dropped an atomic bomb on Nagasaki, Japan, a town of 253,000. That night I learned to ride a boys' bike. Dad rode his own bike in the evenings in the country, and now I could ride with him too. Momentous events, they were for the whole world and for just me—and for Mother, who did not want the devastation of war or the deaths of good men and women and children, especially her boys. She made soap, and she made cake. Life goes on. Her Bible verse she read in the morning for our hearing was Psalm 26:1, "JUDGE me, O Lord; for I have walked in mine integrity. I have trusted also in the LORD; *therefore* I shall not slide." Her faith in God and goodness held firm.

Two days later the Sorenson Warehouse was ablaze. As it was next to the oil tanks along the tracks and the flames were spreading, the neighbors were all pretty scared that the tanks would blow up, and a bunch of them walked over to the club house near us on the edge of town. Dad and Leone stayed near the fire, and Mother thought that I was there, which worried her. I told her later that I was at the fire on our boys' bike and got scared and rode it all the way to the Reuben and Ernest Rasmussen's dairy farm, a mile out of town. So only two days after I learned to ride a boys' bike, I found out that a bike could serve as a quick getaway. Three hours later, when the fire was over with, we all came home and had a very late supper, to Mother's great relief.

I put that bike to more good use, riding the Mason girls around, with Bonnie or Phyllis sitting on the front "boys'" bar or hitched sideways on the back fender and hanging onto the seat. I did some of my errands for Mom on my bike instead of walking, and I rode around "collecting" for Dad and the railroad.

Before Avis left for the fall session of Bob Jones University, we three sisters slept in Dad's newly purchased green trailer house. We had been sleeping in the front upstairs bedroom and sometimes the west bedroom, shifting rooms with the comings and goings of the boys, from the time I was in kindergarten. Now, in the nice warm summer weather, we opened the small screen trailer windows and talked into the wee hours, cozy as clams.

VJ Day occurred on Sunday, September 2, 1945, with the formal signing by Japan of surrender to the United States and our Allies. That effectively ended World War II. There was a palpable relief in our community, and we started a new school year two days later. With Bible school and Chetek Bible Camp behind us, Avis left for Tennessee, Leone began her first year of high school, and I advanced to fifth grade.

The first nine years of my life (and more to come) were seeded by loving parents, grounded in a small community's camaraderie, ethics, and values, and nourished by caring, available people. I was set up for even more learning and growing and soon enough bearing fruit with accomplishment to give back to life on this earth.

As my mother would quote The Apostle Paul saying to the Galatians in chapter 6, verse 7: "Whatsoever a man soweth, that shall he also reap."

Dr. Tyvand

WE WERE A HEALTHY brood, the seven of us kids, for whatever reason. Genes? Good organic vegetables from Mother's garden? A stable, loving home? An ethical and moral base from our parents and from church? Expectations of good behavior, but no cruel pressures or punishments?

All those things made for a healthy psyche for the most part, and for comfortable living in my own skin and in our family's everyday living. We were rarely sick.

But we did have a family doctor in our lives: Dr. Tyvand. We never used his first name, though the sign posted on the outside wall of his two-story, white wooden house on Dewey Street, which he also used as an office, said "Dr. James C. Tyvand."

Dr. Tyvand was a quiet, gentle man, with gray hair and plain eyeglasses. He didn't take up much space with his size, so he was hard to notice on the street. But he made house calls. Dr. J. C. Tyvand, assisted by his nurse, Mrs. J. C. Tyvand, brought my sister and, four years later, me into this life, at my mother's bedside at home.

Mother was the one to see him more than the rest of us did. She agreed with his natural approach to health, and she liked the way he treated her with kindness and patience. She could consult with him about natural remedies for herself and her children, and she rarely got prescriptions for drugs. He was an MD, but he believed in the body healing itself.

Mother used sulfur salve on her skin irritations, rashes, bites, and small wounds. The salve was made by smashing sulfur with a mortar and pestle

90

and adding it to some form of petroleum, like Vaseline or lard. She believed that it helped, and the belief alone may have helped. I got impetigo, a very contagious, crusty, itchy, bacterial infection, on my nose more than once, and Sherman got it on his cheek and chin. The various salves we used, including pink calamine lotion, might have hastened the healing, or maybe the infection just ran its course. Some of us seemed prone to cold sores, and spirits of camphor was at the ready in our small, mirrored, wooden, built-in-the-wall medicine cabinet over the bathroom basin sink. Hydrogen peroxide, too, was always ready to cleanse and oxygenate any open wounds and to use on abrasions. Mom ordered a health lamp from Montgomery Ward to give heat and good energy waves to body parts that needed healing. Besides anemia that she and fourteen-year-old Avis took liver capsules for, she had shortness of breath. Dr. Tyvand came over at Dad's urging, and he ordered her medicine that she said was "supposed to help me." The next day, Leone picked up the tablets, capsules, and powder for thirty-five cents at Fortun's Drug Store. Whatever was in those powders seemed to take care of it—or again, maybe nature just took its course.

Twelve years before I was born, Sherman was born with a clubfoot. Mother, faithfully and "ahead of her time," took Sherm on the trains to Milwaukee on many trips. A local doctor, Dr. Peterson, accompanied Sherm and Mom on the train (we know Dad tried to get the doctor a train pass; if he was not successful, Dad would have paid for a ticket) to see an orthopedic surgeon, Dr. Goenalin, in Milwaukee. He first wrapped the left foot in a soft material to prevent friction, and then he fitted a boot made of plaster of Paris to Sherman's foot. While it was soft and wet, he used pressure on the foot until it dried, and Sherman wore the boot until the next treatment. Eventually the foot straightened out, and Sherm wore shoes with steel shanks for special support, holding the foot rigid and straight into adulthood. It didn't stop him from being a first team forward on the basketball team, golfing, or ski jumping. He asked Ma when I was three if ladies had different feet than men since they wear different-shaped shoes and high heels. Ma said their feet were about the same and that they should wear straight shoes. Then Dallas said, "The store men make them that way. So it is not the ladies' fault."

Dad drove to Arcadia to see a chiropractor for various pains, and he liked it enough to go back several times, but the rest of us didn't go. He was sick with a fever when Leone got Dr. Tyvand to come over. The doctor wanted him in the hospital, but Dad wanted to stay home. He got a first-time antibiotic in March 1947 of penicillin pills, plus ten of what they called "fever pills" for thirty cents. Dr. Tyvand didn't have a cure for Dad's ringing in the ears, and neither did Dr. Simon, the eye, ear, nose, and throat doctor in town, who gave him several "treatments" of unknown description. The treatments didn't help him with his hearing loss and Dr. Simon ordered him a hearing aid. All my life I had to raise my voice and clearly enunciate when I talked with him. It didn't stop him, though, from expressing his views on any subject and sharing his wisdom.

All seven of us did get the big four viral diseases: chicken pox, red measles, German measles, and mumps. They were no respecter of people, and we had no vaccines then to ward those off. Vaccinations for the red measles, German measles, mumps, and chicken pox were not developed until the 1960s or later, so they were too late for our family's use—if our parents would have even chosen for us to have vaccinations. Mother knew what was traveling around and what the signs were for the measles, mumps, and chicken pox. A red-brown rash on the face and body with a fever and sore eyes and throat was how red measles showed up, and we were quarantined for fourteen days. German measles was more benign (unless you were pregnant, when the virus could damage the fetus), with a fever and body aches and sometimes a rash, and you were over it in a few days. You probably had mumps if your jaw, cheeks, and neck were swollen. Chicken pox made for an itchy rash with small red bumps on the scalp that spread to the back and stomach, and you had to wait until all the bumps crusted over before you were considered not contagious. But if there was a question about any of this, Dr. Tyvand made a house call.

We did have some vaccinations, reluctantly on my parents' part. I got two shots for diphtheria and small pox in kindergarten and again in seventh grade, as did Leone. We'd get just enough of those viruses, in a needle, to trigger our immune cells to attack the invader and set up a lifetime of immunity.

We never had those serious diseases or scarlet fever, whooping cough, or typhoid fever in our household. As a public health warning for all of those diseases and for the common childhood contagious ones, doctors put up quarantine signs the size and shape of a folded newspaper on a window or the screen door facing the street to warn passersby. It was like "a pox on you." Those signs are collectors' items now.

That was how contagion was dealt with. You were warned about the killer diseases, you expected to get the common childhood viruses eventually, and then you had immunity for the rest of your life.

Some diseases that you would rarely see today showed up. Our neighbor, Serviceman James DeBow, contracted rheumatic fever in August 1945 and was confined to the US Naval Hospital in Great Lakes, Illinois. One of Aunt Ellen's teacher friends came down with scarlet fever, so they closed many schools. And several relatives got whooping cough, easily spread with the coughing, so they stayed isolated.

Dr. Tyvand and my family knew that good ways of living and good food affected one's health. Exercise mattered, and we all did it easily and naturally in the course of our day, running in games like tag or softball, biking, walking, winter skiing, ice and roller skating, sledding, and hiking at Castle Mound and at Perrot State Park, where the Trempealeau River meets the mighty Mississippi. Dad had books such as *You Are What You Eat* by Victor H. Lindlahr (published in 1940, decades before the modern TV and book version of the same name and different author) that were like bibles to him. He read Bernarr Macfadden's books and followed his health practices, including walking for miles and miles to stimulate the body and brain and eating fresh fruits and vegetables from local farmers and from our own garden. Macfadden, in his books, approved of some meat, and we occasionally ate pork chops, fresh chopped beef made by Ma into meatloaf, and canned tuna and salmon purchased at Foss Store. Mother bought live chickens from Getts Poultry and freshly killed turkey from the Trempealeau County Insane Asylum at Thanksgiving time. A farm with chickens, turkeys, and milk cows on the asylum grounds provided supervised, productive activity for able-bodied patients and made income to support the hospital. Getting rid of toxins was vital, and Dad (but not we kids) did it with fasting and enemas. And at the top of the list was believing in "mind over matter." We heard Dad say "it's mind over matter" almost daily in the normal course of our lives, and it was a philosophy that permeated our beings. Macfadden opposed vaccinations and alcohol. We had no alcohol in our house, partly because of Sarah and Arvid's religious upbringing, but also because they believed it was not good for the body or mind and that it led to unhealthful things. We all had abhorrence of smoking. Mother said that if God intended for you to smoke, he would have put a chimney on your head. The ministers quoted 1 Corinthians 6:19: "What? know ye not that your body is the temple of the Holy Ghost which is in you, which ye have of God, and ye are not your own?" That made sense to all of us.

Dad told us "you are what you eat." He ate a lot of raw food, and Mom gardened mostly organic, sprinkling the soil after the harvest in the fall with wood ashes. The ashes would feed the earth with potassium and other minerals that would in turn feed the next planting. Dad sliced raw onions with his pocketknife at the table and handed a slice to each of us, served on the blade of his knife. We all had turns grinding carrots in the nickel-plated steel hand grinder that we clamped to the edge of the kitchen work table, and we ate the rich, juicy, orange, raw heap—one of Macfadden's favorite foods—almost daily. Mom used ginger, good for digestion, in apple pie and squash pie. Cinnamon, good for colds and whatever else ailed you, went into cocoa and apple pie and applesauce—made from apples that I helped pick with mosquitoes biting (no repellant or poisons used) and out of which I helped peel the worms (no pesticides used)—that Ma made and canned from her own crabapple tree or bought from the inmates at the asylum. Mother seasoned meatballs with sage, good for easing swelling, and she canned meatballs and gravy in quart glass jars. Honey from Dad's beehives soothed the throat with lemon added. If we felt ill, our parents asked themselves and us, "Did your food agree with you?" or speculated, "Maybe the food didn't agree with you."

What good fortune I had to have such conscientious parents and a doctor who supported the natural ways! We kept an icebox on the side porch and didn't buy a small fridge until 1942, when I was six years old. That meant not much room or time to keep things cold. We ate fresh from the garden, and I walked almost daily to the creamery by the seventh hole of the golf course and bought raw milk that they poured into a metal pint can with a cover that I brought along. I carried it home along with cheese and butter. We also had milk delivered to our door by the Rasmussen brothers from their dairy farm. In cold weather we ate what Mother had canned and the produce that we kept in boxes and barrels on the floor in the cool basement cellar. Mother baked our bread, mostly white but sometimes whole grain, with Daniel Webster flour bought by the barrel from the Olson Feed Store and stored in our cool pantry. The warm aroma drew us into the kitchen for a fresh slice with melting butter. She grew radishes, carrots, onions, beets, Swiss chard, black snap beans, yellow and green string beans, lettuce, potatoes, rhubarb, rutabagas, parsley, tomatoes, and cucumbers, and, if the weather cooperated, she put in a second planting of carrots, potatoes, and onion sets to eat fresh and to cook separately or in a soup. She sometimes used a pressure cooker to save the nutrients in less cooking time. Canning was abuzz in the kitchen all summer long, starting with strawberries for sauce and jam and beets in June and continuing on up to prunes and a second crop of carrots and turnips in the fall. She fired up the wood stove for canning on top of the stove, and Leone would bake a cake at the same time to make good use of the heat of the oven. The glass quart Mason jars, filled with vegetables, fruits, and beet pickles, and small, clear, molded glasses with strawberry, grape, and apple jams and jellies showed off an array of appetizing colors and inviting shapes. All were a work of art, Mom having channeled her artistry. She bought fresh fruit in season, like peaches and pears, by the crate or bushel, kept on the side porch where it was cooler, for our eating pleasure as well as for canning. We did revel in baking and eating cakes, pies, cookies, and a rare slice of jellyroll as the punctuation at the end of our nutritional feast, and we all were slim. And when we sat at our big dining room table for meals, we always said a prayer of thanks for our food. I liked that, and I think it put us in a frame of body and mind to feel good about what we took in. All our body chemicals did a top-notch job of digestion and assimilation and were at the ready to get rid of any unknown toxins possibly lurking in the food.

And Mom's flower garden, spread all around the house and beyond, was food for the soul. A long line of mostly purple and a few white lilac bushes bordered the backyard, and large bridal wreath bushes spread their branches on both sides of the entrance in the front of our house. Purple and gold irises, lilies of the valley, dahlias, roses, hollyhocks, heavenly blue morning glories, poppies, zinnias, and balsam flowers (also called Lady's Slipper and Touch-Me-Nots) filled the spaces with color and fragrance. We gave flowers to our neighbors, like lilacs to Mrs. Bautch and others. Our neighbors reciprocated, Patty bringing Mom a bouquet of pansies and Mrs. Hegge bringing us big pink peonies every June from her big peony field on West Street, which we looked out on from our dining room and the side yard. We carried bouquets of poppies and dahlias to friends in the hospital for their wellbeing—there was always someone we knew in the hospital—and we drank in the beauty and variety of the flora plethora for our own health, spiritual uplift, and edification. Matthew 6:28–29 was firmly planted in our memory: "Consider the lilies of the field, how they grow; they toil not, neither do they spin: And yet I say unto you, That even Solomon in all his glory was not arrayed like one of these."

Dr. R. L. MacCornack, living in one of the big, stately houses on Main Street, was the surgeon in town. He was also a Lutheran and a Mason. Rev. Birkeland of the Lutheran Church was against Masons, and Dr. Mac told him that he, the Reverend, had no authority over what he, Dr. Mac, did in his free time. He had a Whitehall Clinic of his own, still standing, behind the depot and was Dr. Tyvand's competition. Dr. Mac was a strong presence with authority to say "we'll operate." But both my parents had an equally strong distaste for any medical intervention, including shots. They preferred Dr. Tyvand's natural healing and kind ways.

None of us had our tonsils removed, though it was recommended fairly commonly. My left knee swelled up overnight when I was in high school, and Dr. Tyvand called it housemaid's knee. He prescribed flesh-colored poultices with the consistency of silly putty for Mother to spread on my knee. An Ace bandage held it in place. But when it was slow to get better, my mother succumbed to seeing Dr. MacCornack at his clinic. She just wanted his opinion. Looking out for my welfare, she asked him what and why, but he was short with her. Since he knew more than she did, how could she question him? And he proceeded to drain my knee of fluid with a needle. It happened so quickly, we could hardly protest.

I'm glad that my mother preferred the human, natural approach to healing that Dr. Tyvand practiced. That was a gift to me that I have favored all my life.

Dr. Tyvand wrote me a note to excuse me from gym while I was recovering from the swollen knee. And that was the last I saw him.

Not long after that, the town learned with a headline in the *Whitehall Times* that Dr. Tyvand and his wife were crossing the railroad tracks in the neighboring town of Independence in their car. They were too late to see or hear the signal or to see the oncoming train. The GB&W engine crashed into their car, and they were both killed instantly.

The quiet soother of ills, who supported with his hands my passage into this world, was now dead. Birth to death—and, like the unseen train approaching, we never know when it's coming. I was sorry to see him go.

Moving Up

THE NEW SCHOOL YEAR, fifth grade for me, began on September 4, 1945, and the war was over. I think most of us were happy to return to the classroom and focus on our studies instead of the latest war news. I was nine years old and glad that my brothers were back home and that our parents didn't have to worry anymore whether they would survive the war.

Mrs. Goldie Holmes, who wore heels and an elegant, dark mink coat the same length as her dress, showing off with flair her legs right at the knee, walked from her house on the other side of Dewey Street on snow and ice to teach fifth and sixth grades until she left at the end of my fifth grade year and Mrs. Lily Reich took over. My friends and I walked past Mrs. Holmes's white, two-story clapboard house with an enclosed porch on our right after crossing the tracks on our shortcut to get to school. Patty and I lit matches at least once on that very path in the sand by the gas tanks just to look at the flame. Fortunately, we didn't light up the gas tanks. Mrs. Holmes "is very nice and she never scolds," I wrote in my diary. In her classroom, art, science, health, and physical education were added as formal subjects, and social studies was broken down into geography and history. I was an avid reader and a good student.

At home I read all The Sugar Creek Gang books that I could borrow or buy by Paul Hutchens, with titles like *The Sugar Creek Gang Flies to Cuba*, which Leone gave me for my tenth birthday, and *The Green Tent Mystery*. I read the whole public library shelf of Grace Livingston Hill books. Mother called fiction "lie stories," but because both these authors were Christian, she let it pass. Dad's at-the-ready stack of books on the table alongside his chair consisted mostly of history, current affairs, philosophy, and religion, and he was fine with any fiction that I read. Seeing the gamut of attitudes from my parents, I was not deterred from reading whatever interested me. But her "lie story" concept stayed in my head early on with a tweak of conscience, and I also saw it as one way of many to view a made-up story. Truth be told, even though I have read ravenously most of the fiction classics—from Daniel Defoe's late-1600s *Moll Flanders*; Jane Austen's *Pride and Prejudice*, written in the late 1700s; and Stendhal's 1830 *The Red and the Black* to most of the novels of Willa Cather, a fellow midwesterner from Nebraska, and Edith Wharton's many historic novels—I am not fond of contemporary fiction. I think I identify with the modern setting more, and I want the truth, not a tale. Perhaps it is my mother's influence, after all, still alive in me.

Dad took off for a week on Monday, September 10 in our green Pontiac, pulling his trailer to travel the Wisconsin byways for a longed-for vacation. Mom said, "If it wasn't for that trailer house behind I would like to go to a few places too while Dad has his vacation, like Hustler, Merrill and that high place near Wausau." But she must have gone into a vacation mode too. On Wednesday, Mrs. Al Stuve from next door rapped on the door, seeing no one moving around the house. Mother had overslept and hurried to get us up and out without breakfast, a first I think, and we got to school in time. After school Patty and I gathered the dried leaves of fall and made "leaf houses," spreading the leaves on her huge front lawn to mark off all the rooms we wished for, as in an architect's drawing, sparking another lifelong interest for me: house plans.

Our piano bench was solid wood —made, stained, and varnished by Mom. The piano, however, was in bad shape, but I still played it. The piano tuner said it would need a lot of work and wouldn't be worth tuning. He fixed one key that did not work and charged fifty cents. I kept playing it, and a couple of years later, Charles M. Headlee from Fountain City worked on it for over half the day, tuning it, doing minor repairs, fixing keys, and putting white ivory on them, for seven dollars. That kept the piano and me going for several more years until my Dad decided to chop it up for firewood. My parents did not replace it. I would have liked a piano of my own, but I took it in stride, playing the church piano when the building was empty and continuing to play for the church's Young People's Society (a weekly Sunday night meeting of all school-age youth), the Dorcas Society, and some of the church services. The lifetime spinster Gladys Rasmussen, the regular pianist, came up to me once while I was at the piano and criticized my playing. I was hurt, but I was clear-headed enough to realize she had some jealousy in her and was trying to build herself up by putting me down.

That hurt dissipated when my parents gave me a new bike, delivered to our door just before my tenth birthday. Marked on the back wheel was "Roadmaster" and "Eclipse Machine Division, Made in Elmira, N.Y. USA." On the paddle gear was written "F 846 76," and those markings were also clearly saved in my diary. On my party day with several friends and Mom's apple pie and chocolate cake, I wrote, "I did not even know I was going to have a birthday party. I am 10 years old. I do not seem like I am 10 years old." Paul Grover got his new bike at the same time, and we rode them together, I wrote in my diary, "very much." A new wicker basket to attach to the handlebars came days later, the better for me to shop for Mom, to collect for my dad, and to carry my schoolbooks and, on Sundays, my Sunday school books and Bible. I walked home with Paul after church in the evening, and we each bought a sack of popcorn. I forgot to put the twenty-five cents in the collection plate.

The church kept us involved in many ways. I had a fear of being in front of groups, but that didn't stop my having to have a first turn at age nine, when I first led Young People's, with more times to come. I made up and wrote out an interview with Bible characters and read it, and even the minister was impressed.

My mother had her own modest ways. While we girls went to the Baptist church on a November Sunday, she went to the Methodist church to hear Rev. Klein, the guest speaker. He was the one who had married Sarah and Arvid on November 21, thirty-one years before. She shook hands with him but did not tell him who she was. I think she took pleasure in keeping it to herself.

Carnival time was in November, and I dressed as an Indian squaw with a gunnysack dress that mother had made for Leone another year and an old Indian blanket over my shoulders. I wore braids just like I did for school. Joyce Herness was a cowgirl. I was the first one on the program. Leone played her French horn in the band and "waited table."

Mrs. Holmes, my fifth grade teacher, came to our Baptist church Christmas program with her husband, who had just been discharged from the service. I was pleased that she was there and could see me on stage. I don't recall any of my other teachers, except Miss Marjorie Harding, my high school English teacher, ever coming to the Baptist church.

As the youngest in our family, now ten years old, I was the one to pass out our gifts on Christmas Eve at home, to play Christmas carols on the piano, and to read the story of Jesus. From Ben and his family, Leone got a "dog pocket book" and I got a "kitty pocket book." It had the markings, size, and rounded shape of a kitty's head in leather, with a zipper rounding the top. I was intrigued enough with it to write a poem, and my mother liked it enough to write "Ethel made this up about her purse" and save the copy that Dad had typed up from my handwriting. I called the kitty a "he" until the last two lines when "he" became a "she." Or maybe Dad made a typo.

WHISKERS
Whiskers is my cat.
His eyes are very green.
When I look at him:
They look very keen.

He really is a purse:
To put my money in.
Sometimes he is fat;
Sometimes he is thin.

I try to keep him fed;
By putting money in.
When she is not full;
She sort of gives a grin.

The snow and ice receded in the New Year, and we knew that spring was on the way when we saw Jack Rhode, the undertaker, on the street wearing his straw hat. On Friday, March 15, 1946, he made his annual appearance. And more good news came via a telegram from Sherman, back in the States from the war on that same Friday and on his way home.

Sherm made it to Whitehall in time to drop Leone and me off at church for a one-time religious rite of passage ceremony for all good Baptists. At 8:00 p.m. on April 14, I was totally immersed in a tank of water in the floor of the altar, and baptized by Rev. Salseth, who stepped down into the water ahead of me. I was the first of ten, including Joyce and the Grover boys, to be tipped way back, with Rev. Salseth holding a handkerchief over our mouths and noses. I said later that "I couldn't remember at all when being dunked under. I wonder if he really did put me under the water, but my hair got wet, so he must have." With my fear of water, maybe I went into a transcendent state, appropriate for a baptism, to block out the fear. I also feared that I didn't really believe the dogmas that all this entailed. I was uncomfortable with the uncertainties. It was a heavy psychological load for my ten-year-old psyche to handle. But my mother said I was a pretty happy girl. And she was probably right too. It was a ceremony that I happily survived with my friends. A week later I joined the Baptist church as an official member.

On April 29, 1946, while I was out playing at night, I saw a big star that looked nearly as big as the sun. Then it got scattered into several little stars.

I told Mom and she recorded it in her diary, but neither one of us read any sign into it that I remember. The moon was a waning crescent at twenty-seven days old. Mercury, Venus, and Saturn were in the evening sky but were not in a confluence. My parents kept track of eclipses of the moon and sun for us to watch. I loved looking to the sky for all the years I can remember and would call Mom and Leone out to look at rainbows. In October 1944, less than two years before I saw the big star scatter and at the end of a rainy day with the sun breaking through, I told Mom and Leone to come out and see the pretty rainbow. "And is it ever pretty," Ma said. "It looks so it extends from ground to ground and north and south, the Rainbow being on the east side of house toward Stuve's." Then, seeing the big star get scattered into several little stars in '46 kept me fascinated with the heavens and looking for other mysterious sky happenings ever since.

On a beautiful day in May, Mom commented, "The birds are singing so nice." And they looked colorful too—the yellow crowned bobolinks, mottled brown meadowlarks, and scarlet tanagers sharing tree space with the Baltimore orioles and the chickadee.

Dal and Sherm, both full-time wage earners now, took Dad, Mom, Leone, and me to the Walgert Hotel for supper. Once in a great while there was reason to dine out, but mostly we counted our pennies and didn't splurge on a restaurant. I ordered a T-bone steak at $1.20 and pie that cost an extra seventy cents. That was a treat. Sherm probably said his trademark phrase, "what a deal," with a crack of a smile that expected us to be amused. We were. He also said "what a deal" if something didn't work out the way you wanted it to. And it lightened the disappointment.

When the Grover and Herness boys got the red measles and I started coughing in early in June, my mom expected that I was coming down with the measles too. Any discomfort and suffering with the fever and red pimples on my face dissipated with all the attention it brought. Mrs. Stuve, Avis, and my dad brought me a quart of root beer from the Club House for being sick, Audrey and Clarice came over with two cut-out doll books and licorice sticks, and Patricia Hegge brought a bouquet of nice big roses. I was so happy about it all—I didn't know having the measles would bring me all those things. My "red, pimpled face was all smiles about it," my mom said.

It was July of '46 when Dad took a break from his heavy load at the depot to become agent in Alma Center to rest and recover and live in his trailer house. I rode the train on Saturdays to see him and to "collect" from the local businesses there. Leone came also to clean the depot windows. Mother came on the train to be with him and visit relatives. Then, back home in Whitehall, Mother made tuna fish and peas in a cream sauce on toast for our supper with our neighborhood friends.

With fall and cool weather approaching, Mother ordered two loads of poplar wood for the kitchen cook stove from Ardell Paulson, dumped in a heap by the driveway for us to pile under the garage eave and to stack in the basement come winter. She also got three loads of coal for the furnace, delivered and dumped onto a chute that angled down through an opening to the basement coal room. When the trap door on the opening couldn't be locked until they were through dumping coal, a big rat must have come in. Mother heard that rat for the next month and finally borrowed a cat from her sisters that caught the rat in the basement one month later. She was "soo" glad that it was gone.

Mrs. Lily Reich was the new teacher for fifth and sixth grades, and I entered sixth grade on September 3. She wore her dark hair combed up to a nest on top of her head, rimless glasses on her pretty face, a dark suit to midcalf, and heels, looking very much the prim and proper school teacher. I liked school, and I liked her very much. Mrs. Reich started the safety patrol, and we all had a turn at it. A wide, white webbing strap crossed our chests diagonally and went around our waists, and we took turns standing at the curb with a sign to alert cars to kids crossing the road.

Church and school continued to occupy a big piece of time and focus in our lives. The kind, soft-spoken Rev. Salseth and his family left that fall of '46 to go back to school in Upland, Indiana, to become missionaries in some faraway place on the globe. Special speakers came to the Baptist church on Sundays until the new minister, Rev. Jacob F. Waechter, was ordained and installed many months later. He became my Sunday school teacher, and he didn't like my questions about the theology he knew best. Bravely for me, the obedient soul, my internal questioning was slipping out, and the responses I got didn't align with my logical thinking. But I remained loyal on many fronts.

With an artist's palette of colors, Rev. Salseth, our former pastor, chose his chalk and oil paints for his landscapes, and Mother's artistic muse picked a variety of colors, from maroon to teal blue in boxes of Rit Dye, to dye rags for colorful rugs and to give new life to old clothes. She dyed my gold coat blue on my eleventh birthday and made a blueberry pie, an apple pie, and two pumpkin pies. She set the pies aside when the neighbors took a bunch of us to Mrs. William Olson and my friend Roger's farm in the country in the afternoon, and they gave me a surprise party of angel food cake, potato salad, Jell-O with banana slices embedded just under the surface and topped with whipped cream, sandwiches, milk, and coffee for the grownups. Our family ate Mom's celebratory pies for me the rest of the week.

Trigger, a black cocker spaniel that my father bought, lived with Dad in his trailer in Alma Center and at home in Whitehall for about half a year. In January 1947, Trigger got several spasms throughout the day. Dr. Lamberson and Dr. Reichenback both looked at him and didn't think he had much chance of pulling through. For several days, he had convulsions, and then he seemed to come to life and walked around. Then he was played out, with light attacks during his sleep. Dr. Reichenback gave him shots for nourishment, but he died in our dining room. It was probably distemper. He was not immunized. Seeing his black shaking body lying in a curl on a pad and putting my hand gently on the side of his body made a lasting imprint on my brain. Dad, and the others, and I felt so bad. Aunt Emma's boyfriend Oscar took Trigger home to bury on his farm, where he could dig in the ground under snow. The ground in our garden was too frozen. Trigger, in his short lifetime, hadn't been able to catch that rat in the basement.

I was just eleven when I was elected president of the Baptist Young People's in January 1947. Sherman came to give us a talk on India, which he did with ease and humor. As leader of the BYP's, I somehow squelched my fear of talking in front of a group. I had sung and played piano in front of a congregation for years, but if the fear rose, I would get a lump in my throat. For a morning service, Mrs. Herness, Joyce, Leone, and I, with Rev. Waechter on the right end, were lined up and sang as a quintet on the stage in front of the churchgoers. One of those lumps briefly clogged my throat, and I missed a word as I swallowed and tried to keep singing. The Reverend—how ever could he be revered?—bent down to me slightly when we had a break in the song and in an angry whisper said, "Don't you ever do that again." Of course, that just made me more scared, but I made it through the song. Humiliation is not a good way to encourage a healthy pursuit—as with Miss Lentz while learning "time" or with Rev. Waechter, who was the Baptist minister for most of the rest of my growing-up years in Whitehall.

The fifth and sixth grade school picnic closing the 1947 school year was on May 29. Joyce, Howard Grover, and I all brought baked beans. If there were any gassy repercussions, we marched it off the next day. Memorial Day was the march to the cemetery. Leone was in her band uniform with her French horn, I just marched along with the parade, and our brothers Sherman and Dallas marched proudly in their soldier and marine uniforms, with Dallas in the fire squadron. Later in the day they played in a golf tournament at the club house.

School was barely over, and vacation Bible school began. This two-week string of mornings in the sanctuary and the classrooms of the Baptist church provided the yearly ecumenical display of the Methodists, Lutherans, Tabernacle, and un-churched, as well as the Baptists. It ended with all of us having parts in a colorful closing program, played to a full church.

War rationing ended June 10. Mother was able to can with sugar again, and Dad was very glad to get a five-pound bag of sugar from Mom for his trailer in Alma Center. The strawberries were nearly ripe, and Alma Center called itself the strawberry capital of the world. I became a serious strawberry picker that summer of '47, picking ten quarts for our family for $1.25 in a day in Dad's adopted town and then in Henrik's fields from dawn to dusk for them to sell. I almost fainted with the sun and heat. As my head was swirling, someone told me to sit with my head tipped way down. The days were much too long, and we picked day after day, probably without drinking enough water. Our family later called it slave labor. And Dallas's work on the section crew through the summer was hot and hard work, which wore the men out and sometimes made them sick. Among other injuries and illnesses, Dal got an infected blister on his finger while handling the tools and lumber ties, developed blood poisoning, and had to get "gas" (general anesthesia inhaled) and an operation in the hospital.

I started babysitting with a varying wage of fifteen to twenty cents an hour. Sometimes I had to stay awake until two in the morning, painful for an eleven-year-old. We were all getting jobs at something to earn money and eventually take care of ourselves. Dad tried to be enterprising in addition to being a depot agent. He started building birdcages in his workshop, intending to breed yellow canaries and sell them. He made a trip to La Crosse to buy one male and four female canaries, the male costing $10.25 and the females $2.25 apiece. One could measure value in different ways, but did that measure of value resemble the human culture and the roles we play? We girls did the work of cleaning cages and feeding the birds. Some baby birds were born, but they slowly died off, as did Dad's short-lived hopes for a new business. With the death of the canary business, Dad took up honeybees. The honey business was a little more promising. He built frames and boxes in the basement and bought hives of bees from other parts of the country and had them shipped home on the train. He bought Dasher's used bee equipment very cheap and built up a couple of dozen hives, and the next year had several dozen more. The honey flow was good after the rains. I went out to the hives with him to watch him work in his veiled hat and thick gloves, and I helped him extract honey from the framed combs in a centrifugal extraction drum, which was set up in our garage, that I spun with a crank on the side. We all sold the quart jars to whomever we could. In the winter Dad covered the hives with tarpaper to help keep them alive.

Avis gave me my first permanent wave, a "Toni wave," in July, so it was goodbye to my French braids that I was happy with all my childhood years and that had kept my hair out of my face and out of all of my activities. Curls were a new look for me at Bible camp. Dad, with his usual humor, wrote me on July 25, 1947, from his depot in "Punkin Centervilleson, New Jersey. USA ... I see by your card you need CASH. How would 50 cts do? Here it is. Maybe you will not receive this before you leave. If not, Leone will probably get it, so it will still be in the family....Suppose you go in swimming every day. Do you get your suit wet? ... A.B.E. Uncle Abe the old side Kick."

I began my last two years of grade school in the fall of 1947. Mom picked a fall bouquet, as she did every fall, along the tracks and welcomed Dad home from his year in Alma Center. Well rested, and his health regained, Dad drove his Pontiac with the trailer hitched behind, bringing his bed/couch, radio, and typewriter home and was ready to take up his job again as agent in Whitehall. Mom said, "Will seem nice to have him home with us. So nice for all of us." Church activities filled the weeks for Leone and me, with Rev. Waechter hosting frequent social times for us kids and having us "roll tracts" to spread the Word of God wherever we chose to leave them. I remember once leaving a tract very self-consciously and uncomfortably on the bench inside the La Crosse bus station, and I do not think I made any other "drops." Imposing on the unsuspecting a creed that I felt uncertain about anyway did not suit me. Mother had me take bundles of our out-grown clothes to the Baptist church for the needy in Europe. That suited me much better. And Mother got five pounds of fabric remnants from Sears for her (and me) to sew more clothes. "Were they ever good," she said and got down on her knees and thanked God for them. At the same time, she was going to church less—never to the Tabernacle and hardly ever to the Dorcas Society or to church services. Was her fervor wavering? She said that she'd been doing plenty at home and that that was enough, with her resting a lot and feeling weak. And we had a reminder of the ever-present danger of the farming business that fall when Carl Janke lost his hand in a corn shredder and was taken to the Black River Falls Hospital and when Alfred Dahl had part of his fingers cut off and crushed in a corn shredder at Richard Erickson's farm.

But school was the steady structure of our days and lives. Mrs. Arleen Bensend taught seventh and eighth grades in the west corner room facing Dewey Street. Math, English, reading, spelling, social studies, and science were the basics of our learning. We had music, art, home economics for the girls and industrial arts for the boys, taught as separate subjects with different teachers than our regular classroom teacher. Making an apron was the big project for us girls in home ec, and I had to rein in my creative ways with scissors and machine sewing that I had exercised since I was a preschooler. We had to measure exactly the length and width of the parts of an apron to cut the cotton fabric with precision, baste a thread through our measured markings at the top width to make gathers, and then figure out how to carefully sew all the parts together in the right order on the black electric sewing machines in consoles lined up across the classroom, next to the practice kitchen. I felt tense with the notion of getting it all exactly right and then being evaluated by the teacher. It wasn't fun like my sewing used to be. I was judged by the very serious, straitlaced Evelyn Suomi, receiving a B– despite having sewed almost all my young life. Art also was structured with guidelines for drawing and painting a landscape, and what we created was then being judged on which was best. Joyce won first place. Where did that leave the rest of us? Fortunately, I rose above that feeling of not measuring up, and I flourished with sewing projects and a full breath of art media for many decades to come. And music was a joy to brighten all my days.

Mrs. Bensend, who taught all our basic subjects, had a petite figure and short, clipped, dark hair and was wonderfully brisk paced in her reading and talking about anything. And she was smart. You believed her without question, and you wanted to be like her. She really put us to work and said it was in preparation for high school. Most important for us, she opened all our eyes to the wonders of life by reading the book *Mrs. Mike*. It was a love story based on the life of Katherine Mary Flannigan and held us captive with the young woman's resilience and bravery. It was our course in sex education. We didn't get it in science class, and you certainly did not talk about it. An expression people used, "loose lips could sink ships," could apply to a lot of things, including sex. Saying too much could lead to problems. If you talked about someone having "sex," it could hurt his or her reputation. But we sat in rapt attention whenever we finished our class work and she picked up the hardcover book, standing in front of the class and reading about a young Boston woman's falling in love with a Canadian Mountie and moving to the Northern Alberta wilderness. We were enchanted. I didn't need anything else in my two years with Mrs. Bensend but that classic book by Benedict and Nancy Freedman written in 1947, the very first year we were lucky enough to have Mrs. Bensend.

That summer of 1948, I won second place for my 4-H club entry in the Trempealeau County Fair. I had bought two yards, at forty-nine cents a yard, of a yellow (my favorite color), small-flowered cotton print, at the Farmers Store. Mom got me started with the cutting, and I sewed it into a pinafore, fitted at the waist with a tie. I did measure up after all.

Principal Gus Boll resigned, and C. S. Edwards became supervising principal in the fall of 1948. I was eager for another year of learning with Mrs. Bensend. My eighth and last grade of elementary school flew. When Christmas vacation came, Leone and I took the bus to Winona and the Chicago, Milwaukee, St. Paul, and Pacific Railroad train to the big city of Minneapolis to visit our big sister Avis for a few days. She cooked for us and took us to see the sites, including the Pillsbury Building, home then of the largest flourmill in the world. But the frosting on the cake was our afternoon of music. We went to St. Paul, the other Twin City, to hear Yehudi Menuhin play the violin with the symphony orchestra. I was transfixed with the size of the concert hall and the beauty and perfection of the music and inspired to do more with my music. Leone must have been inspired too.

When we returned home to begin school again in January 1949, she started playing the saw. She held the handle of the saw in her left hand and the blade between her knees. With her right hand she held a violin bow and played the smooth edge of the saw like one would bow the strings of a violin. She changed the notes and created a vibrato by bending the saw blade up and down with her left hand, and I accompanied her on the piano. We played "I Am a Pilgrim, I Am a Stranger" for services at the Baptist church and the Tabernacle and for anyone around who wanted to listen. Plus we sang duets, Leone singing alto and me soprano. Sometimes we switched parts.

At the end of eighth grade, our class went on a trip through Trempealeau County. We hiked up Trempealeau Mountain and visited what used to be Gale College. We saw it as a Catholic novitiate to train young brothers and priests in Galesville. Being a Catholic in Whitehall seemed an oddity, so it was good for my friend Joan Hunter, who had just moved to Whitehall, to have her religion given some attention.

Leone graduated from high school in May 1949, I finished eighth grade, and the summer vacation flew. In late August, Leone and I took the Chicago and Northwestern train to Janesville to spend a week with a bunch of our cousins on my dad's side of our family. I loved to play the Carlsons' beautiful Hammond electronic organ, reaching for the foot pedals and using both keyboards, for what must have been hours at a time until Uncle Harold came into the music room and sternly told me to stop. He did enjoy music played by his daughter Evelyn, the concert-pianist-to-be, and he would not have disapproved of the music I played. I think he didn't want me to wear out his organ. I had a pit in my stomach and a big lump in my throat to think that I had done something wrong, whatever it was—I still don't know. I thought I was putting the organ to good use. To counter that admonition, Aunt Martha was so sweet, and I spent time with my favorite soul mate cousin in the Erickson branch, Neil Erickson. Leone and I returned home on the train, ready to immerse ourselves in new school experiences. Mother said that she missed me, as I was usually so good about doing the shopping.

Leone went to the Luther Hospital in Eau Claire to become a registered nurse and eventually a nursing instructor at the University of Wisconsin–Milwaukee. I moved upstairs in the brown-brick school building to the third floor, where all my brothers and sisters had spent four years of high school, to become a freshman in September 1949 and share space with the upperclassmen.

The Coulees

"COME, LET'S GO FOR a ride in the coulees," my dad would say when he was free and the sun was still up, and off we'd go in his car with the windows down through the rolling hills outside of town. Whoever was around plus a friend or two, or a special relative like Uncle Harry from Norway, would climb into his 1938 green Ford Deluxe four-door sedan, later a couple of playful years in a black Dodge coupe with a rumble seat, and then a green Pontiac, with Dad sitting comfortably at the wheel.

We had the good fortune of living in unique geological terrain of hills and valleys that the French settlers called coulees, from the French word *couler*, "to flow." Tributary streams flowed through the coulee valleys to the Wisconsin, Saint Croix, and Mississippi Rivers. As the streams and rivers approached the Mississippi, their canyons grew steeper and deeper to their mouths, as high as 1,700 feet. The coulee region, extending from western Wisconsin into northeast Iowa, northwest Illinois, and southwest Minnesota, came about because the glaciers did not come here. The great ice sheets of the last (and current with Greenland and Antarctic ice sheets) ice age started two and a half million years ago and peaked eighteen thousand years ago, grinding out of the north, passed to the west and east of coulee country. The ice planed the land in its way, carved out the Great Lakes, and, as it retreated, it left behind "drift" of silt, clay, sand, gravel, and boulders that overlay the solid bedrock. But coulee country was left "driftless" because the glaciers passed us by. The melt water flowing from the glaciers, however, made its way to the streams of the valleys in the coulees. Left alone with a half million years of erosion, the coulees were filled with trees. With farming in the 1800s, the ridge tops and valleys partly turned into pastures and row crops, and they retained beauteous views.

Dad knew this, being the self-taught student of history, geography, and all things curious that he was. And he loved "the beautiful scenery among those hills." He relished philosophizing and expounding on the history and the beauty of the landscape and on religion and the grand scheme of things. I loved to listen to him and sometimes asked questions to elicit even more of his thinking, considered by many people in Whitehall to be unusual but was admired and humored—except by the Baptists, who considered his thinking heretical. He would not be going to heaven with those beliefs, and they were hell-bent on rescuing him from his own follies. I was an admirer.

There were at least a dozen coulees within an easy drive of Whitehall and neighboring towns. There were no signs to tell us the names. We just learned over time, like colloquial phrases, the spoken names attached to the coulees surrounding us. Thompson Coulee, Sjuggerud Coulee, and Dissmore Coulee were all northeast off US Highway 53 on the way to Pigeon Falls. Dad kept some of his beehives near two Dissmore houses in the coulee named after them and in Sjuggerud Coulee, named after the Sjuggeruds, both not far from the city dump. I made trips out to those coulees with Dad when he needed to tend to his bees. The bees fed off the fields of clover and other flowering crops, and they pollinated thousands of acres, irrespective of vague coulee borders, to help keep agriculture alive.

The big ski scaffold, where I watched my brothers jump in freezing weather, was in Thompson Coulee, which had an especially high hill. We drove up the steeper rise to a grand view of rolling hills for miles around on County Roads D, O, and E. We might go by the hamlets of Hale, Pleasantville, and Elk Creek to wind west and south on State Highway 121 to the small town of Independence, home to Maule Coulee and Swede Valley—there were a few Swedes like us in this mostly Norwegian and Polish territory. From Independence, Dad could head home through Packer Coulee or drive a straight five miles staying on 121. That took us past the Trempealeau County Hospital, a couple miles west of Whitehall. Visiting the asylum, as we usually called it (or, by a more common phrase, the insane asylum), was a separate trip. Dad would pull in the very long driveway that edged a vast expanse of lawn scattered with tall shade oak and maple and evergreen trees on the left. Ahead of us was the several-story brown-brick building that housed the inmates. We parked along the shale road and lounged on the grass or on the wooden lawn chairs and benches spread around the green, but not close to the highway. The inmates roamed around, all in similar dress, and acted strangely, very much unto themselves. I felt no fear. I observed the oddness and found the whole milieu wonderfully calm and peaceful. We communed with nature, and Dad held forth with me alone or with whoever came with us in the car on his philosophical views about people, the world in peace, and the universe. After an hour or two or more of a timeless spell, we drove home to a supper that Mom had ready to put on the table.

A coulee ride was twisty with switchbacks, and Dad drove slowly up and down and around the hills to take in the ever-changing view. There was nary another car on the road. At high points, Dad would stop for us to get out, stretch, walk, and drink in the expanse of gently rolling hills.

Other coulees we visited were Steg Coulee north of and Tuff Coulee east of Pigeon Falls. Turri Coulee, Tappen Coulee, and Voss Coulee were all east of Blair. Big Slough Coulee, Curran Coulee, Fall Coulee, and Trump Coulee were all in the area of the small towns of Taylor and Hixton, where some of my mother's relatives lived.

Irving Coulee, as we all called it (today some shorten it to "Irvin"), was our favorite place to ride. The paved and then gravel road south of town curved and wrapped around rolling fields of green corn and grasses. The crops stood in a wide swath that was elegant to behold. Climbing slowly, past banks and large clusters of towering oak, maple, and elm, we reached the high point, the top of all the hills in sight, where the road ran along the edge of the hill. Down below was what my dad called "the most beautiful scenery I have ever seen." He had traveled all over the states on the trains but said "it beats California, Florida, Minnesota and all the rest of the USA."

I was entranced. My mind was swirling with the wonderment of the earth, the heavens, and my place in it all. Dad waxed philosophical, and, in the quiet beauty, he felt even freer and more inspired to express his beliefs. I was as young as eight years old when he described the electron as a spiritual substance, its orbit covering the entire universe. The mind as composed of matter of a much finer substance that vibrates at a much higher rate. All matter is made of the same substance, the differences being in its rates of vibration. The mind is a part of our spiritual makeup, probably contained in our soul. The subconscious minds, whose existence has been established by clairvoyance, is also a part of it, as it contains all that we have ever learned, said, and thought in times past. He articulated that with our knowledge accumulated and experience gained, the individuality, the personality, and all characteristics, good and bad alike, and the spiritual, moral, and intellectual attainments are fundamental to the evolution of mankind as it marches toward betterment from generation to generation, from life to life, through eons of time. Nothing is destroyed or wasted; everything merely changes its form of existence. That includes human life and the individual Ego and all phases and planes of nature.

Both Dad and I had experienced the wonders of nature in the coulees—rainstorms with lightning and cracks of thunder that thrilled me, the covering of winter white that glistened in the sun, seeing the moon in all its phases as the sunlight was fading, and the unfolding of spring.

We stopped to pick wild roses along the side of the byways of this coulee region. Dad said, "Wild flowers, all kinds are now coming into bloom throughout the countryside. Roses are the first to show themselves. You probably have heard the song, 'the last rose of summer;' these are the first roses of summer … the end of their period of hibernation as they emerge, take root again and show us what they can do in the matter of renewal of life and form. It is an age old process that applies to all life on our globe, human, animal, vegetable and even mineral life."

In late August, with fall showing and frequent drives, as Dad described it, "over the winding roads and hills through the coulees and valleys surrounding Whitehall, one finds that the forested hills are ablaze with colors as though the trees were on fire. Along the streams in the low lands the sumac and the ferns are the first to turn brown; then the colors reach up to the maples and other trees until all are in flaming and living colors. Leaping from crown to crown of the forests, the colors race up the slopes of the hills to the top and spread in all directions, as the green of summer slowly gives way to all the colors of the rainbow. The most conspicuous are the maples as they put on a spectacular display of pastels, brown, gold and yellow that rivals the best a human artist can reproduce. The oaks and the poppies are the last to be touched with nature's color scheme and their contrasting green make the display of the maples and other trees the more beautiful. Nature thus shows herself in her glory of gold, red, orange and yellow with patches of brilliant pink on treetops and extending to the ground, all of it splashed with hues that shine like glowing coals. In the morning when the sun reappears, the mists rise slowly and reveal thousands of new and different color schemes in the hills, in the valleys and roadsides, the colored leaves falling and mingling with the still green grass below, adding to the beauty of the scene. Science has established that all these colors were in the leaves all summer long; that the green produced by chlorophyll predominated and covered them up until the diminishing heat of the sun in the fall causes the green to slowly disappear, revealing the bright colors beneath."

We were both filled with awe at the splendor, and Dad wove that admiration back into religion and the Bible. He attested that "if one follows the instructions as given in the 'Sermon on the Mount,' by Jesus, we need not be concerned about beliefs and creeds. That is principally what he (Jesus) came here for, to show us how to live in order to advance, or to acquire the virtues, or to perfect ourselves as much as possible in order to inherit the good things in store for us in the next life. The human Soul, being indestructible, having always existed, is not for that reason subject to salvation or destruction. On the contrary, I think it is subject to improvement ... As I understand it, the Soul is a spark of the Divine, which has always existed."

My dad could share his views for hours if there was time or type for pages if he was writing letters to family or to a special correspondent and old friend, Mr. Thaddeus Parr, another philosopher at heart, living in another city, who could jostle him in a written sparring match. They kept it up for many years.

The sun was setting when Dad drove home. Whenever he got philosophical and had carried on for a while, he said it was time for him to stop, get down to the business of everyday humdrum of life, and carry on as usual.

We did go back to the business of the everyday, like church, school, and work—but with a richer awareness of life and a better sense of the expanding and exciting possibilities of answering those big cosmic questions. I was born with a heavy dose of curiosity, and I loved the journey even more, sharing it with the parents and family that I had, with the moral support of the church, living and learning in the idyllic town of Whitehall from birth to age seventeen.

ℋigh School

My FIRST WEEK OF high school, in the autumn of 1949, the circus came to town, and I went with Joyce to see elephants, clowns, and trapeze artists perform tricks in a tent behind the Land O'Lakes Milk Plant. My dad also came to see the show, and Mother walked there alone just to see the crowd and went back home. She said, "It seems empty around the house with all of them gone." It was down to just my parents and me.

I was told by the upperclassmen to dress as Columbus for freshman student initiation day, but unlike the circus performers, I did not have to show off any tricks. I did have, in my words, "very much fun ... as well as embarrassment." I knew, though, from my Scandinavian heritage, that Leif Ericson discovered America in 1000 AD, way before Columbus, born in what is now Italy and sailing on behalf of the Spanish Crown, made it here in 1492.

Leone, the horn player, was now gone, and I was encouraged to take up the mantle and study the French horn in her stead. I loved the horn and the music, so Mr. John Whitney, with a good-looking head of thick black hair, and later Mr. O. B. Renslo became my teachers and bandleaders. I also joined the orchestra, playing my newly taken-up stringed instrument, the viola. For performances, I had the lovely pleasure of wearing a long yellow formal that Mother made with a boat neckline and fitted waist. Like the inspiring Yehudi Menuhin, I was playing a bowed instrument, just as Leone had with the saw. I sang either soprano or alto, as the need arose in Miss Betty Dunne's and later Mrs. Jerry Nelson's chorus and glee club, all of us wearing robes.

Mrs. Bensend had prepared us for high school with our hard work and gave us some idea about the hormonal urges and surges to come with the reading of Mrs. Mike. It wasn't such a mystery anymore. Our hormones were starting to kick in, and the attractions were coalescing. I got my "monthlys," as Mom called and spelled it, for the first time as a freshman at age fourteen, on February 1, 1950. I remember sitting at my desk in study hall and feeling wetness in my underpants. I made it through the rest of the day with the help of toilet paper and without too much show. Having two older sisters gave me some awareness of what it might be. They used white muslin rags that were washed and reused to catch the flow, and about twenty-eight days later I was better prepared.

The hormonal urges manifested as attractions to boys that had just been buddies of mine in grade school. Another layer of being with them was developing. There were boys I especially liked, but being a Baptist did put a damper on things. The Baptists forbade dancing, makeup, and drinking alcohol, so that ruled out a big social opportunity to get teasingly close to a guy. My "wayward" brother Dallas did get away with being prom king his junior year, though he didn't dance that we heard about, but we girls felt that we had to toe the line more stringently. Leone did help decorate for the prom, but Mom said she could not serve juice on the night of the prom. Though she had promised, they got someone else to serve. Also, the boys that we were interested in might not be "saved," which we were taught was important to have in a mate. So I imagined them, probably very unrealistically, getting down on their hands and knees and accepting the Lord as their savior. I really enjoyed guys and was social with them, and we did projects together—particularly the smart and funny ones, like the droll Dick Duebert who always sat next to me or in front of me, an Erickson, in the classroom alphabetical order. Paul Grover, my childhood Baptist and biking buddy who traveled on the first team for basketball, adventurously got a girlfriend at Blair High School. There weren't any other Baptist guys my age or ones that I liked. I settled for crushes. I didn't date or have a kiss all through my high school years.

On the girl front, a group of six was coalescing in my class with my grade school friends, Sharon, Mary, Rita, Susie, Shirley Mae, and Kari Lynn. We all called them "the clique." They called themselves "the gang." In common, they had the Lutheran church (though Sharon was Methodist), dancing (Rev. Birkland was against it but the Lutherans still danced), and a big interest in boys, like our classmate Rolfe Johnstad, the musically talented, handsome, and what-should-I-do-but-be-merry brother of Dal's buddy Connie. I didn't fit in with that, though I would have liked to still be friends. There was a little feeling of being left out. But then I had a sort of clique of my own. Joyce Herness, my best friend from the cradle on, and Joan Hunter, newly arrived the end of grade school and sort of an outsider as a Catholic, and I became pals, and we helped run things along with the gang. We were editors or reporters on the *Whitonian* newspaper and *The Echo* yearbook, active in sundry clubs, performers in many musical groups, and achievers academically. Members of the gang were also cheerleaders and twirlers, and after school hours they had boyfriends, some from out of town, and they hung out socially. My own group of three hung out in the *Whitehall Times* office, a small, white, one-story building at the head of Dewey Street and Main, next to the expansive lawn of City Hall. Joan's mother worked there, and we were given her cast-off books of Plato and Socrates and history that we took turns choosing as our own. We worked on class projects together at my house, and we had platonic relationships with Dick Duebert and, behind us in classes, Roger Erickson and David Wood, all smart, fun people to have verbal repartee, philosophizing talks, and laughs with in study hall while working on our writing projects for anything and everything in the school.

I loved school and all my teachers and was pretty much an A student all four years of high school. The academics more than befitted me, and I was at one with the music. Mr. Jahn Tinglum, handsome and always dressed in a suit and tie with a clip, was my favorite teacher, and science and math, which he taught, were my favorite subjects. General science started my freshman year. Mr. Tinglum—*How could we be so lucky?* I wondered—taught science with such knowledge and clarity that I was hooked. I took it all in like a hungry creature, wanting to learn as much as I could about my world. And I had a crush on him that he never knew about.

Miss Marjorie Harding taught freshman English. How kind and nice and pretty she was! Tailored blouses and suits, skirts midcalf length, and an occasional punctuation of a flared skirt comprised her fashion. My eyes were drawn to an array of shoes, flats and heels that carried her through a week or two without repeat. She was the leader of the debate team, which I joined. I wore brown, shiny leather loafers and white anklets, a light blue fitted wool skirt with a box pleat in the front to just below the knee, a short-sleeved light blue lambs wool sweater, and a small dark blue silk scarf tied around my neck. Words were Miss Harding's thing and mine too. She had us write autobiographies, and mine was titled "Remembering." I cut each letter out of a magazine picture of a baby and glued the letters diagonally down a blue construction sheet of paper. Inside were five pages of hand-scripted stories of my life and a last page of three pictures arranged diagonally down the page: one of me as a baby, a second of our family of nine lined up diagonally, like a partially open deck of cards spread out in front of the tall spruce trees, with me at around four on the left end, impishly tipping the top half of my body way over to the picture's left, and the third of me, around five, standing in a short dress, buckle shoes and anklets, bangs covering my right eye looking into the sun, and arms hitched behind my back. She gave me an A+ and said, "I like this story of your life! Well told. Keep this." Thank you, Miss Harding. I did keep it and I hope you like this one too.

The staid, unexcitable teacher of industrial arts for boys, Joseph G. Emerton, also taught business training in a mundane way, which was meant to prepare us for the practical mathematical dealings and business of everyday life—if your mind wasn't elsewhere. He did tell me to do as well for the next three years, so I must have been paying at least a little attention. Football and basketball coach Carroll Lohr taught citizenship, which covered history and social responsibility. I supported his sports teams by playing my horn in the pep band and marching in uniform on the football field at halftime.

Mother, never a queen for a day (which our neighbor watched on TV), wore a royal blue formal and long royal gloves befitting a queen, her first long dress since her wedding dress, as mother of the groom in Sherman's wedding to Eva, who was of 100 percent Swedish heritage. We took the train to Minneapolis early in February 1950, had days of festivities, and then returned to our normal lives. The fish in its fishbowl died from the cold, but the Bautches took care of the one canary we had left from Dad's failed bird enterprise, who thus survived, at least for a while more. In April, we had a good old-fashioned midwestern all-day storm with heavy rain, thunder, and lightning. The light bulb in the kitchen burned out just as both Mom and I saw lightning go through the kitchen into the dining room. We all survived.

As soon as school was over at the end of May, I biked to Joyce's farm, and we both biked some more to have a picnic in the woods. The glorious summer days were here again. Three days later, we gathered friends and played volleyball on the Hernesses' vast yard. I liked to serve the ball, even though it stung my clenched right hand. Dad picked me up on Sunday afternoon, along with my bike, and he taught me how to drive the car in the coulees. What a thrill it was to be at the wheel and have my patient dad show me a skill that my mother and her sisters (except for Aunt Ellen, the teacher) and a lot of other women in their generation did not have! We got home in time for me to go to evening church and join Joyce and Gwen to sing the Swedish song translated to English, "He the Pearly Gates Will Open," as a trio. for the evening service: "So that I may enter in, for He purchased my redemption and forgave me all my sin." The next week we started an orchestra with other musicians in the church. I played both viola and French horn, and Joyce played cello and trumpet. Music was a lynchpin of our church, as well as our town.

After vacation Bible school in July, our family again made use of our free train passes and took a trip to California, climbing the hills of San Francisco by foot and cable car, which even Mom said "sure was fun," and riding the peaks and dips of the wooden roller coaster in Santa Cruz.

Mr. R. M. Bungum took over from C. S. Edwards as principal of the school in September 1950, my sophomore year. The band and orchestra leader, Mr. John Whitney, also taught us world history. It was a mighty thick book then, and there has been so much recorded history since. However do we keep up? And I was the happiest model student in two of Jahn H. Tinglum's classes. Biology was a live science, which I favored over other sciences, and we dissected dead frogs. He introduced us to the theory of evolution. Vera Thompson, a Baptist mom whose farm I went to many times to play with Gwen, did not approve of our being taught evolution like it was a fact. In her mind, it didn't agree with the Bible's teachings. No one that I knew of, to my relief, made any formal protest to the school, and I was glad to get my knowledge from Mr. Tinglum. I was disagreeing more and more with the Baptist theology. My other class with Mr. Tinglum was algebra. What could have been a jumble if taught by someone else made absolute sense to me with his ordered presentation. I still had a crush on him.

Dad had spent the past months building a miniature replica of the Baptist Church, several feet square, in his free time. It was to be our Christmas decoration, sitting on the snow-covered lawn. He used wood and cardboard and painted it white. Mother made people dolls out of fabric and wood to sit inside the church and to stand outside on the lawn. With its charming belfry and clear windows, all lit up, and white snow to show it off, it looked like the real thing. I helped Dad set it up off to the side with a Christmas tree and lights. On December 23, Dr. S. W. Simonson came to our house while we were eating supper and told us that we had won first place on our church and decorations. He awarded us fifteen dollars. Willie Johnson across the street won second place and ten dollars, and Ed Gardner won five dollars for third place. Even though Dad didn't go to church, the rest of us did, and he felt enough fondness for the place to build a small replica and show it off to the town.

The New Year, 1951, was a continuation of the old, with the same classes and teachers challenging us to learn more, choral, band, and orchestra musical performances with and for many groups, and after-school jobs. We started going to regional and state contests with our horns. It was remarkable to have four French horn players, all sophomores, in the band, and Mr. Whitney and then Mr. Renslo showcased us. Mary Ellen Thorson, Lorene Hanevold, Rachel Almlie, and I made up a French horn quartet that traveled to Ensemble Day in La Crosse and placed in contests. Mary Ellen and I went to the state contest in Madison for solo and duet performances. I got carsick on the way down to the capitol and had to do a fast recovery. We played in the education building on campus. Rachel wrote in my 1953 graduation yearbook, "remember the 'fun' we had playing after beats, transposing music, climbing over Roger to put our horns away, & bickering about whose turn it was to put away the music ... then too there was our talented French Horn Quartet & our solos at La Crosse ... Love, Rachel." The summer came with more jobs and time with friends, and fall arrived.

I was a junior now at age fifteen and learning Latin as part of the triad with Joyce and Joan, and alongside Rita, Sharon, Mary, Susie, Shirley Mae, and Kari Lynn of the gang, we had a treasure of a teacher, Mrs. Sylvia Rice. She brought out the best in us with her sweetness, firmness, and charm. We repeated the demonstrative pronouns *hic haec hoc* and *huius huius huius* out loud time after time till it seemed almost musical. We sang songs in Latin and felt learned like the priests in my friend Joan's Catholic world. "*Aut viam inveniam aut faciam,* I shall either find a way, or I shall make one," Mrs. Rice wrote me. "I am confident that success would crown your efforts."

Chemistry with Glen Olson, wearing a black vinyl bib apron over his shirt with rolled-up sleeves, tie, and pants, was not a "live" science, and I didn't fare as well—plus I felt like the teacher, who mainly taught agriculture, didn't know what he was talking about, making it tough to learn. But I did manage a B+ in difficult terrain. Elvira wrote in my yearbook, "That was one class I didn't learn a thing in." But Mr. Olson was a nice, gentle man, and I babysat his kids in a house that looked just like ours but was two houses down from the school on Dewey Street.

Instead of going to the junior prom in the spring of 1952, I worked for the Berdan's in their Berdan Floral Shop on the south side of town. Leone used to do it, and I took over when she left for nursing school. Starting the day before the prom, I put wires in leaves and flower stems, twisted green floral tape around them to have ready for corsage making, and put them in the big cooler with glass doors. Gardenias, with their strong, heavenly aroma, white, yellow, and red roses, and other flowers and leaves filled the space. The next day I helped with putting them together, but Ken and Clara Berdan "created" the corsages. I checked the guys' names on the orders and wished that I could be asked to the prom and go and dance, but I knew it wouldn't happen. I felt a little blue to be making corsages for people I knew and not be able to go myself. And I also wondered about the Berdans, who were Baptists too, having even a business part in the prom. If you believe any of it, where do you draw the line? The lines of principles and dos and don'ts were hazy for me, and it was tempting to shed them all. Charles Jacobson (the new boy in fourth grade) and Rita Olson, my junior classmates, both deserving of something special in my mind, were the king and queen of the prom with a Chinatown theme. I could only imagine the lovely strapless gowns with corsages that I helped make pinned at the waist or worn on the wrist, the swirling on the floor, and the music of a small live orchestra from out of town. And on Monday I was back to my classes, like I hadn't missed a thing, to finish up the year.

I took the train to Saint Louis Park, a rich suburb of Minneapolis, to be a nursemaid for the summer in the Brooks household with two small children in my charge. Like the lower-class help, I slept in the basement of the regal-looking stone house on a hill and observed and learned about the sophisticated world of moneyed social climbers. The experience was good for a story I wrote about Teddy and Jane, my charges, for Miss Joan Pitzner's English class that fall and was good as well for the A that she gave me.

It was the beginning of my last year at Whitehall High in 1952. I was a senior with aspirations, and I had work to do. College was on the horizon. Mrs. Sara Keeler of the College of Saint Theresa in Winona brought her own brand of sophistication to Whitehall High, with her intelligence and awareness of the ways of the world in my Social Problems class. I hung on every observation that came out of her small, red-lipsticked mouth. The rest of her was an elegant gray: her subtle gray plaid, fitted, and belted suit with a row of large black buttons and highlighted with a pointed white V-neck collar resting neatly on the top; heels; and her silver, graying, wavy hair combed back to fully frame and expose her face. I studied the surface and could almost see the store of information deep in her brain as she imparted her knowledge. We never used texts. It all came out of her head. I was ready for a teacher like her, and it was the send-off I needed and wanted for what was ahead. David Wood, our platonic pal and a junior, got special permission to be in that class of all seniors. We thought that he liked our class more than his own. Mrs. Keeler once called him the most insipid person she knew. Dave, who later became an author and a columnist for the *Minneapolis Tribune* and the *Whitehall Times* and who was adept with words, asked her what that meant. Having a second year of Latin with Mrs. Rice was a bonus, and I was rewarded with an A+.

Dwight D. Eisenhower was elected president of the United States on November 4, 1952. Dad had picked him to win in a letter he wrote to me at Bible camp back in July. He also wrote, "Ike, I think, is a 'man of destiny,' just like F D Roosevelt was and as several other men in history have been, such as Lincoln." Once in a good while, Dad did vote Republican instead of Democrat. That year Mother and Dad's votes were the same.

On Christmas of 1952, Dad typed a message on a telegram from the depot and handed it to me. "Ethel M. Erickson...On this your last Christmas of your Happy High School Days, I wish for you a future of promise and expectations. May your striving for them be as happy as their realization. Love...A.B.E...."

A third of our triad, Joan Hunter, was going off to Mrs. Keeler's Catholic college, and among all the sentimental, praising comments that we all wrote to each other at the end of the year, Joan said the sweetest: "You're honest, God-fearing and God-loving. You're loyal and true and steady. And what's meant the most to me – you've got a sense of humor. College is going to be pretty strange for me without you around, Eth, to lean on and laugh with. Best of luck and may the Good Lord always grant you what you want most. Always, Joan. P.S. Pretty sticky, huh?" And there was a full page more from her, budding writers that we both were.

Joyce was accepted at Wheaton College. I got a scholarship to North Park College in Chicago and eventually earned a degree at the University of Wisconsin–Madison.

Joyce and I had the same horoscope, written in our high school annual, the *Echo*, for "best friend." She had me, and I had her. Her favorite pastime was painting, and mine reading. Her hobby was oil painting, and mine French horn. My ambition was to be something, and Joyce's to go to Europe. We accomplished both.

My name was the next to last of forty-two in our senior class prophecy. "I was sorry to see what a failure Ethel Erickson had become. After being such a fine high school student, she ended up riding the trains and begging for food at each stop." It was a fitting ending to my school days. The trains were a central part of my life, and both the writer and I had a sense of humor to carry us through our days to come.

A baccalaureate service in the Lutheran church gave us a religious sendoff, and the class of 1953 graduated on Thursday, May 28. Commencement exercises were held in the school gymnasium at 8:00 p.m. We left the halls of Whitehall High School and moved on to a life beyond the small, familiar, fun, and happy place we had been so lucky to grace. Dad called my graduation a "'red-letter' day in our tribe as she was the last of the brood to do so. Seven graduating nights over a period from 1925 to 1953 makes a lot of history in one family!"

The renewal of life in the May spring bloom of our town and surrounding coulees, in the church's celebration of the resurrection, and in the bursting of all new life made me look eagerly to the future. I took my past life with me as I rolled onward and forward like the trains. As a last hurrah to my depot- and rail-centered childhood, I rode the rails on the Chicago and Northwestern Railroad to Chicago and college and a new life.